Anything Is Possible

Also by Alan Epstein

How to Be Happier Day by Day

How to Have More Love in Your Life

Anything Is
POSSIBLE

Real-Life Tales and
Universal Lessons

ALAN EPSTEIN

VIKING

VIKING

Published by the Penguin Group
Penguin Books USA Inc., 375 Hudson Street,
New York, New York 10014, U.S.A.
Penguin Books Ltd, 27 Wrights Lane,
London W8 5TZ, England
Penguin Books Australia Ltd, Ringwood,
Victoria, Australia
Penguin Books Canada Ltd, 10 Alcorn Avenue,
Toronto, Ontario, Canada M4V 3B2
Penguin Books (N.Z.) Ltd, 182–190 Wairau Road,
Auckland 10, New Zealand

Penguin Books Ltd, Registered Offices:
Harmondsworth, Middlesex, England

First published in 1997 by Viking Penguin,
a division of Penguin Books USA Inc.

1   3   5   7   9   10   8   6   4   2

LIBRARY OF CONGRESS CATALOGING IN PUBLICATION DATA
Epstein, Alan, 1949–
Anything is possible : real-life tales and universal lessons /
by Alan Epstein.
p.   cm.
ISBN 0-670-87447-7 (alk. paper)
1. Life change events—Psychological aspects.   2. Life change events—
Psychological aspects—Case studies.   3. Adjustment (Psychology)—
Case studies.   I. Title.
BF637.L53E67 1997
155.2′4—dc20   96–43985

This book is printed on acid-free paper.

∞

Printed in the United States of America
Set in Granjon
Designed by Junie Lee

For my family

Acknowledgments

I WOULD LIKE to thank my agent, Patti Breitman, for sticking by me through thick and thin; my editor, Carolyn Carlson, for challenging me to do better; and my wife, Diane Epstein, for reading draft after draft and somehow getting me to put aside my resistance and see the light.

These episodes touch upon the most basic emotional aspects of human existence, the hopes and fears, memories and desires, crises and milestones that represent the colorful threads that, when woven together, form the tapestry of being. Each person weaves his or her experience with the threads of his or her own stories, the particular incidents and developments that define that person's uniqueness.

Anything Is Possible consists of twelve such stories. They are arranged chronologically, and, taken together, they fill up a large area of my own personal mosaic. They are important to me not only because I remember them vividly, but because I have been able to derive meaning from them. And they can be significant to you because perhaps by learning about the ups and downs and ins and outs of my life you can make better sense of your own.

I have chosen the title of the book for a variety of reasons. First, in the widest sense, it reflects the Americanness of my experience, a reflection of the great, enduring optimism that is at the core of the signature principles of the country—our emphasis on life, liberty, and the pursuit of happiness. As I see it, to think that anything is possible is to think like an American.

Second, the title reflects my view that no matter how carefully we tailor our course of action to fit our goals and objectives, circumstances always arise that compel a series of improvisations that really, finally, determine whether we live successfully or not.

Third—and most important—*anything is possible* is my

Introduction

As a freshman in college thirty years ago, I first came across Socrates' conviction that the unexamined life is not worth living. While I can't recall the impact it had on me then, in retrospect I can readily see how much that little phrase penetrated my consciousness.

In truth, I have made examination—of my motives, growth, the unique way in which my experience has taken shape—an abiding principle around which my life is organized. This predilection to examine, combined with my intensive training as a historian—which taught me how to give form to the usual morass of detail and circumstance that is the essence of anyone's experience—has prompted me here to try to interpret various episodes of my life as illuminating tales of growing from childhood through adolescence into adult life. Reading about my experiences as an ordinary person growing up in America in the second half of the twentieth century will, I hope, inspire you to examine your life in a similar way.

Contents

Anything Is Possible

1

Homeward

Bound

IT WAS MIDWAY into December of the first year at a new Hebrew school, and the day began under leaden skies. As I dunked my white toast into my cup of half instant coffee and half milk, reading the sports page of the Sunday paper, I heard my father say that he was going to take his galoshes to work because the weather forecasters were calling for snow.

My ears perked up at his remark because for a child growing up on the East Coast the arrival of snow was more than just another meteorological phenomenon—it was an event. Whenever snow was forecast, there was always the possibility of a *snowstorm,* which might result in the closing of school, which to my mind was the greatest gift God could bestow. It wasn't so much the opportunity to go out and romp around in the cold white stuff that so delighted me, although that would have been reason enough; it was the unexpected that so stirred my imagination. Snow meant for me release from the routine, the possibility that the day might turn out to be different from the way I had gone to bed the night before thinking—even *knowing*—it would be. It was fate's messenger, bringing the news that things were not *always* going to turn out the way they had been planned, and that during the winter months there was always the credible threat that a cold nor'easter would barrel up the Atlantic coast and leave such a thick white blanket in its wake that the authorities in charge would have no choice but to close the schools until the streets could be safely plowed or salted.

In fact, the ritual of gathering around the radio with my parents early in the morning after snow had fallen the night before, to await our respective fates, was one of the tensest, most anxiety-producing moments I can remember as a child. There was never any doubt my prayers were being countered with equal fervor by those of my mother and father, whose days would certainly not go as planned if I were to be home from school. And if the entire scene was reminiscent of a dramatic moment in some B movie, the moments before the expected announcement were couched in almost biblical terms for me. Whose heartfelt imprecations would God answer, my parents', pleading for order, or mine, advocating chaos? And when the broadcaster suddenly made everything in the household stop as he began to list the various school closings, the tension among us became almost unbearable. As I heard him say "All Philadelphia public and parochial schools will be . . . ," I shut my eyes to await the verdict. And so on the days when I heard the announcer utter the word "closed," as sacred a word as there was in the entire English language for me, I would erupt in excitement and joy that *my* prayers were the ones that got through, and I would ignore the looks that flashed between my parents, which were the opening salvos of their negotiation as to which one of them was going to be inconvenienced that day while I was receiving my gift from the heavens—in more ways than one.

But on this bleak, cold Sunday morning in December 1960, not a single pristine, six-pointed crystal had fallen, and I had learned not to get too excited about snow until it had in fact begun to fall. So when I piled into my father's car to be dropped off at Hebrew school on his way to work at the women's clothing store my parents owned and operated, which was at that time in our lives open for business on Sundays, my thoughts were not so much on the possibility of impending snow as they were on the fact that I had choir practice that morning and would thus be out of the classroom for a while—singing, which to me was better than being in the classroom, reading the *Chumash* (Bible reading) or copying passages of text in my *machberes* (notebook).

What's more, choir was in a different building on the campus of my school, so I could even get out into the bracing winter air before finishing class for the day, and get back home by hopping on the C bus on Broad Street and the J bus on Lindley Avenue in time to watch most of the Philadelphia Eagles football game on television. This was really in the forefront of my mind, since the team had won nine games in a row and had already clinched a spot in the championship slated for later that month. But watching the games on TV was a treat in those days, as far fewer contests were televised.

Bubby, my grandmother, with whom we lived, would welcome me home from *Cheder* (Hebrew school) with a piping
hot bowl of chicken soup, whose aroma would permeate every
nook and cranny of the house, and I would settle in to spend a
few hours watching my beloved Birds.

The choir sounded particularly good that day. It was led by a
handsome young teacher named, of all things, Mr. Paradise,
and he prodded and cajoled us to dig down deep into our
souls and sing as if we were speaking directly to God. The
songs he had chosen for our recital, which was coming up soon,
were beautiful, haunting melodies that we harmonized to perfection. My participation made me realize that not only listening to popular love songs on the record player and the radio
but singing itself could take me beyond my usual range of
emotions, to places I didn't experience often, that certain notes
would set off feelings of longing, inspiration, belonging, or extraordinary beauty. It was moving to follow the effusive Mr.
Paradise, obviously passionate about the music, pushing this
motley group of eleven- and twelve-year-olds to do better, to
pay attention, to visualize the sound and then let our voices be
guided by the harmonic dignity of the Hebrew notes. By the
time our practice had ended, it had turned into an emotional
experience. The group had sounded good—even to my cal-
low, untrained ear.

When we walked back to our regular classes, nature's
show had begun. The streets were a canvas of one wind-
driven color—white. Although the snow had been falling for

only fifteen or twenty minutes, the early indications were that this would develop into a major storm. For one thing, the snow was light, dry, and easily whipped by gusts of wind that were beginning to slap at my face from the Northeast with punishing regularity. Snow that didn't amount to much was usually wet and heavy, and often melted as soon as it fell on the asphalt or paved concrete. But this snow was already developing into something thick, insistent, and ubiquitous, and the temperature seemed about five degrees lower than it had been when I left my house two hours earlier. The sheer volume of flakes began to create a world of white, covering everything. It wasn't long before the force of the storm persuaded the school's officials to send us home early, as conditions outside were worsening by the minute.

I quickly boarded a C bus and watched the storm intensify as we slowly made our way south on Broad Street. All the while I knew I was in for a treat. This snowfall would be one that I'd watch from within the warmth of my house. Even after dark I could spend hours with my younger brother gazing through the cold, rattling glass of the windows at both the front and back ends of the house, watching the snow accumulate, standing guard at the slow unfolding of this spectacular drama that might culminate with the coveted word "closed" being heard on the radio in the morning. As I got off the bus at Lindley Avenue to transfer to the J, I was ecstatic. The temperature was 20 degrees, the wind was blowing about 30 miles an hour, gusting and swirling the snow in every direction, and in a few minutes the J bus would come by and drop me off a few feet from home, where I would enjoy its comfort and familiarity, shielded from the fierce elements that were now raging around me.

I was fortunate to be waiting for the bus under a railroad bridge, where I could shelter myself. But I was beginning to wonder about my good fortune. When the bus failed to arrive on schedule I didn't make too much of it, as that happened occasionally, but when the second and third buses did not show either, after an hour had passed and the snow had deepened, the temperature had dropped even further, and the wind was fiercer, I knew I was in trouble. My parents were working, Bubby was at home and didn't drive, and even though I was only a mile from our house, it seemed to me that I could have been in another galaxy. I had walked home from this spot many times before, but never in six inches of snow. And my fear of the unknown, my inability to make a decision about what to do had the effect of freezing me inside to such an extent that it made the outside of me seem warm by comparison.

I just couldn't see a way to get home. I kept looking across Broad Street to see if the bus was there, incredulous that the Philadelphia Transportation Company would choose this time above all others to let me down. My mind refused to believe that the bus would not come. My faith in the predictability of life was sacrosanct. It didn't matter that a snowstorm was now in full force—the bus was supposed to take me home and in a few minutes it would arrive. I knew I could make it home by foot, but that could be painful and uncomfortable. My fingers and toes might get frostbitten, and the gale force winds might make it difficult to breathe. Watching snow from the relative tranquillity of one's house and playing in it after it had stopped falling was one thing. Walking a mile through a raging blizzard was another. I kept thinking, God, why did you put me in this position? How am I going to get home? What do I do? What do I do? Please help me decide what to do. I'm only eleven years old. Where is that bus? Where is that darn bus?

I was frozen to the spot. I worried that if I did start walking and a bus passed me, I would have missed my ticket to safety. Bus drivers were notorious for ignoring passengers if they were not waiting at the yellow bus stop signs, and I think my heart would have sunk clear out of my being if I were to be en route while one of the green vehicles passed by. This is what buses were for, for the times when you couldn't get a ride in a car. And even if I was at a stop when the bus happened to pass by, there was no guarantee that the driver would let me stay on, since I had a transfer from the C bus and transfers were good only at transfer points and I didn't have another token. What if he wouldn't let me stay? I was already near tears. Would I be able to hold back from crying?

I realized then that if I decided to set off on foot, I was committed to that course of action. There would be no turning back. I was going to have to make it home alone. There was no one to call, no car or bus or taxi to drop me off at my front door. At a certain point I realized that if I did not make a move, I would be in the same spot all day. Time was passing, the bus wasn't coming, the football game was on, and instead of being home watching it, I was standing under a railroad bridge like a baby, waiting for a bus that obviously wasn't coming.

As soon as I left the relative protection of the bridge, my feelings of terror, which were as palpable to me as anything I had ever experienced, vanished, teaching me a valuable lesson that I have never forgotten and which has become a personal mantra—"Action is the antidote to anxiety." Another way of saying this is "A step in any direction is a step in the right direction," and my first step out into the muffled fury of this winter snowstorm relieved me immediately of the anxiety I had endured unremittingly for the previous hour. Within thirty seconds of the start of my foray into the bitter cold, I had the confidence to make it home. It was merely a matter of putting one foot in front of the other—something I had learned to do ten years before—until I was at my front door.

After a block or two a feeling of exhilaration set in. I was lonely and tired and scared, but the knowledge that I would be home in a matter of minutes comforted me. The numbered streets seemed to come and go with increasing rapidity, and I actually felt stronger as my walk progressed. It was a revelation to realize that I could brave the elements if I had to, that I too was not without strength, endurance, and courage. I was not a baby anymore. This snowstorm was now as fierce as any I could remember, and here I was, out alone in the deserted city streets, determined to get home and in front of the television to have soup and hot chocolate and watch a football game.

As I turned the corner of my street, congratulating myself that I had accomplished what I set out to do, I realized that no

J bus had passed during my journey. I would have still been standing at the corner of Broad and Lindley, waiting for assistance that never would have arrived, frozen in fear in the frigid conditions, my terror inside contributing to the cold outside, watching my hope for salvation diminish with each passing moment. I had taken off into the unknown. I had been true to the tenth of the Boy Scout commandments—to be brave—and had been rewarded with a memorable experience that only added to my sense of being able to endure extreme conditions and survive them, to meet a physical challenge and overcome it.

Bubby helped me remove my frozen clothes as I settled down in front of the tube to watch the Eagles lose a meaningless game in the same conditions I had just moments before navigated. This was a big storm—it was even snowing in Pittsburgh, two hundred and fifty miles to the west. Bubby chided me gently about not calling to tell her where I was.

"Vwat heppened?" Bubby asked, in heavily accented English. "I vass verried about you."

"The bus didn't come, Bub," I responded, trying to eat, watch the game, and be polite at the same time.

"Vy didn't you call and tell me vair you ver?"

"I thought of it, but I was afraid I'd miss the bus when I was in the phone booth."

She felt my head. "Vell, you don't heff a fever." She then realized that my attention was elsewhere, and lapsed into Yiddish resignation as she disappeared into the kitchen. "Ball ahene, ball ahair." (Ball here, ball there.)

It snowed all through the day and and by early evening it

was clear to everyone in the household that tomorrow's verdict was going to go in favor of the children. The snow continued through the night, and by morning fifteen inches had fallen on city streets that had been clear the morning before, making it one of Philadelphia's heaviest snowfalls; the failure of officials to order the snowplows out on the streets early enough made the task of clearing them all but impossible. School was closed for three days, the longest stretch of unexpected vacation that ever materialized in the thirteen years I spent as a student in Philadelphia, and the storm was a harbinger of the fierce winter that followed. Six weeks later, on January 19, the East Coast was again buried by heavy snow, and while most citizens remember President Kennedy the next day delivering the call to "ask what you can do for your country," I was out with my trusty shovel, earning $12 to clean off the steps and sidewalk of four houses at $3 per house. Politics didn't mean that much to me at that age, even the inauguration of the youngest man to be elected President of the United States.

My sojourn through the blizzard marked a passage for me. I realized that paralysis brought on by fear could be overcome through action, that it was no longer necessary to look to my mother, father, or grandmother to take care of every little need, every inconvenience or difficult situation. I was older, wiser, tougher, braver, more capable than I had ever been before, and my setting off into inhospitable conditions proved it to me.

Years later I found myself in a similar situation. A trip to Montreal during Christmas vacation when I was eighteen years old found a group of us enjoying a winter frolic in the Laurentian Mountains north of the city. Snow fell steadily all day as we skiied, sledded, and drove snowmobiles, and the bus that took us back to our host homes in town dropped us off far from where we were staying. The snow on our clothes had melted on the warm ride back, and when we started to walk to our destination—a decision we made immediately and decisively—the four of us knew we were in for an adventure, one that as teenagers we welcomed. Within a few blocks, however, it was clear that our journey would be no picnic. Our clothes froze solidly on our bodies, and conditions were worse than I remembered them to be seven years earlier. It was dark, we hardly knew where we were going, and the walk tested our levels of endurance.

But while I can't speak for my three companions, I do know that what sustained me, what made my journey that day palatable, even delicious, was the memory of my solitary expedition through the cold, snowy streets of my hometown. I had done this before. I was practiced, experienced, and perhaps the meaning of that Sunday when I was eleven was that fate knew it had a very difficult three-mile walk in store for me in the future, and that it afforded me the opportunity to experience myself in action almost as a dry run, as a prelude to an event that would challenge my stamina even further. Yes, I was older, and yes, I was not alone, but at the same time I could tell that I was enjoying this adventure infinitely more than my companions, and that had to be because I had accepted the challenge several years earlier, that I had tested my endurance as a child and passed with distinction, and now as a young adult of eighteen, frozen, stiff, tired, feeling the biting wind blowing dry crystals of snow against my face and body, I could think of nothing but Bubby's nurturing solicitations, the three days of snow that turned into a five-day weekend, and the knowledge that the process of growing up includes the ability to weather the inevitable storms that will develop.

When you see young animals in the wild, their playful tumbling takes place close to the mother. Cubs roll around within sight of Mama Bear. But once the cub disappears for stretches at a time, the mother's reaction is not to scold the youngster but to realize that her cub is getting ready to live as an independent adult. What was significant about my episode in the snow is that for the first time I was dealing with a situation that had me out in the wide, wide world; that I was no longer within the confines of my own neighborhood or venturing out of it only with adult supervision. The fact that I was capable of attending a school miles from my home, and that it was easy for me to take public transportation alone after school meant that I was physically and emotionally prepared to get home even when circumstances like inclement weather forced me to make my way in a different manner than usual.

This is why the most important words uttered by a politician in this century are Franklin Delano Roosevelt's evocation of courage in the face of economic difficulty—"The only thing we have to fear is fear itself." It is the motivation to press on in the face of hardship, of difficulty, of despair that challenges us as a species, that is the stuff of which our greatest stories of triumph are made. And of course we never know in life when we will be called upon to confront something fearful, when circumstances will conspire to present us with a challenge that is unique and formidable. It may consist of doing the multiplication of fractions in elementary school, or giving a speech before strangers, or dealing with a sticky situation in a foreign country as an adult. But whatever or whenever it is, the way we handle it will certainly etch itself on our character in incalculable ways, and become an unmistakable signpost that marks our development as individuals in a constant state of evolution, of becoming.

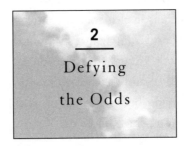

2

Defying

the Odds

RITES OF PASSAGE in adulthood are often difficult to identify, but in childhood they are usually more obvious; leaving behind elementary school and entering junior high—the graduation from sixth to seventh grade, going from being among the oldest students in the school to the youngest—was certainly significant for me. I began attending the Jay Cooke Junior High School in February 1961—in those days students entered school each half year—and as that winter would have it, we were dismissed early on the very first day of classes because of the third major snowstorm of the season, a howling blizzard that was the nastiest of the three. But nature is nothing if not strange, and the storm had the immediate effect of ending fourteen straight days of subfreezing temperatures, and the more long-term consequence of ushering in a spell of milder weather that produced an early and glorious spring. Before long, the heavy snows of the winter were forgotten, and the blooming activities of the following season were everywhere in evidence. For me, that meant ball; and what ball meant, above all, was the unfolding drama of events that one could influence but never fully control.

The game was baseball, but ironically the only time I ever saw the actual granddaddy of games played was at the major league level—either on television or at the ballpark itself. Little league did take place not far from where I lived, but somehow the concrete and asphalt of our immediate urban terrain lent itself to more homegrown and guerrilla games that sprouted right out of the streets and driveways of our neighborhood.

Most of the games were played with a palm-size rubber ball filled with air, called a pimple ball because it was studded with small round protrusions to give the holder a better grip. A pimple ball in those days cost between ten and twelve cents, depending on the quality, and it was considered cool to have had and used a ball for so long that it had eventually become smooth. At that point there would be a little ceremony among the kids I played with, inducting the ball into the Pimple Ball Hall of Fame. Occasionally I persuaded my father to treat me to a *box* of balls, twelve in all, because they were even cheaper by the dozen and there would always be a supply on hand whenever the ball I perpetually carried in my pocket got lost, went down the sewer, or ended up on someone's roof, where it stayed until one of the fathers on the block went up to fix something and walked the length of the roofs of the row houses, throwing down balls that had accumulated over time. It didn't take me long to notice that the balls I bought singly seemed to last longer. The balls that made it into the Hall of

Fame were almost never from a box, as this variety seemed to disappear much more quickly. There was something about knowing that there were more balls waiting in the wings that made me less diligent about keeping track of the one I was using. My father would periodically ask me how many of the twelve balls he had bought for me remained, and he was usually chagrined by my answer, vowing not to buy another box, a vow that would last only until the following summer.

We played a variety of games: stickball—a pimple ball and a sawed-off broom handle; halfball—a pimple ball cut in half and a broom handle; wallball—a pimple ball thrown against the wall of a house; wireball—a pimple ball thrown up to hit overhead wires (if you hit a wire and the other player didn't catch the ball, it was a home run); blockball—you had to get the ball into certain concrete squares on the sidewalk; stepball (aka stoopball)—a pimple ball was tossed against someone's front steps and where the ball landed determined whether the throw was a single, double, etc.; chink (no offense to anyone intended)—a game very much like the indoor game of handball; and handball—the game we played that was closest to actual baseball, in which there was no pitcher, but rather each hitter slugging the pimple ball with his closed fist and running the bases.

All these games were very imaginative, but the ultimate street game, the Game of Games, was boxball. It was like handball, but it had the advantage of having only two players on a side, which was often the number of kids available at any one time. Even though the spaces in which we played were much smaller, it still made sense to play handball only when there were at least three on a side. With fewer available players, the game of choice was boxball.

Boxball was handball—with one important difference. If the struck ball flew above the knees, you were out. It was that simple. It was a brilliant game, singularly designed for small spaces and few players. In effect, it was a game of grounders. Very few players had the strength to strike a ball with their fists through the infield on a fly without the ball soaring above the knees, especially after the ball was in use for a few days, when it lost its initial zip and didn't travel as far or as fast. To accomplish this feat would be tantamount to a major leaguer hitting a home run that leaves the ballpark at eye level. It's been done, but probably only by mythical figures like Babe Ruth—and only in the movies. To me, at age eleven or twelve, boxball was more than a game—it was life. All the drama of competition, of testing one's mettle against the mettle of others, of recognizing the importance of teamwork and communication, of trying hard until the contest was over was played out in the Game of Games.

Boxball was an exercise of controlled tension. Two fielders could cover most of the paved field, so games were usually low-scoring and close. It was not uncommon to go into extra innings, and it was a leveling, democratic game because the strength of the bigger boys, of which I was not one, was of no avail in an undertaking that actually penalized strength. You could hit the ball as hard as you wanted—unless it went above the knees on the fly.

Boxball was so popular in my youth that it was an organized intramural sport at Cooke Junior High, and each section was invited to assemble its own team and compete against the other sections in a spring tournament. Since our field was the school yard, we could play no other game. Any attempt at handball, which made some sense since we could field nine players, was futile, since every hitter would have smashed each at-bat out of the yard and into the street, displeasing the school authorities. And so the game of choice—as usual—was boxball, which I had played every summer since I was six or seven.

Our section, 7A-2, organized its team. Students who had begun the year in September were now in the B sections, and the schools at that time unapologetically "tracked" kids—that is, grouped them according to performance and potential. The "2" sections of each school year contained the "smartest" kids, and in a junior high environment, when adolescent hormones were beginning to emerge, that was not considered cool. It was assumed that smart kids were nerds, geeks, bookworms, Goody Two-shoes types, and so when we began to compete in the boxball tournament, little was expected of our section. The 7A kids were the youngest in the school—in most cases twelve-year-olds—and being the brainiest and the youngest *at the same time* was like the kiss of death. No one, least of all ourselves, took us seriously.

Every baseball team has a manager. When it came time to select one, I was the nearly unanimous choice, which surprised me. Although I had known some of my classmates from elementary school, most of the kids were strangers to me, and I was by no means the biggest, the coolest, the best dressed, or the most athletic kid in the class, and I at first was not interested in the role. But my teammates prevailed, and when we informed our section adviser that I would be the manager, I could sense that the choice took him aback as well.

I was selected because it was clear to my teammates that I was a student of the game—which was in fact the case. Baseball is a sport that lends itself to study, in a way that the other major sports do not. Football is about speed and strength; basketball about quickness, jumping ability, and stamina; hockey about toughness and endurance. But baseball is a game for scholars, a game of strategy, of numbers, of statistics, of lore. If you take the time to really watch and examine the game, you soon realize that there is a pause between every play, which begins when the pitcher throws the ball toward the catcher while the hitter decides whether to swing at it. It is in these gaps that the game is played in the heads of the managers. As in chess and billiards, a decision made now will often have great impact on the action later. Everyone who has played pool beyond the beginning level knows that whether the struck ball falls in the pocket is only half the story—where the cue ball ends up is the other half. If it's in a good position to make the next shot, the previous shot was a good one; if it isn't, it wasn't.

It's the same with baseball. Setting up play so that you give your team the best opportunity to win in the late innings is what makes a good manager, and I quickly learned that there was more to the job than deciding who would play what positions, and what the batting order would be. I learned that a manager is a motivator, and what my teammates saw in me before I could see it in myself is that I am a motivator, that somehow either through my example or cleverness or a combination of both, people want to do their best around me.

Every afternoon at school a flier would be distributed and read to all classes, describing the news and events of interest. On the days following the games we played, there was no greater feeling than to sit and listen to Mrs. Phillips, the social studies teacher, or Mr. Dickstein, our English teacher, read the summary of 7A-2's glories. "Peter Goodman's five hits and three RBI's helped 7A-2 defeat 7A-6, 6–4, in the boxball league," or "Alan Epstein's single with the bases loaded in the tenth inning propelled 7A-2 over 7A-1, 2–1, in yesterday's boxball play."

Our team was rapidly turning into an extraordinary personal adventure, a dream come true for me. Baseball had been my passion ever since I was a small boy, and I had dreamed about being a major leaguer even though I was told by everyone around me that Jewish kids did not play baseball at that level, except for Hank Greenberg in the thirties, and a young, rising star for the Brooklyn Dodgers named Sandy Koufax, who went on to become arguably the greatest pitcher of the modern era. But that didn't matter to me. My dreams of glory, of transcending my background and becoming immortal, were connected to baseball, and now I was turning into something of a hero—the manager of a team of seventh graders who were themselves overachieving, a master psychologist who could deflect other teams' attempts at intimidation through pluck, self-assurance, and focus.

To keep the team motivated, I persuaded some of the more popular girls in the class to come out and support us, to be our cheerleaders. This was a masterstroke because I had remembered from street playing that we all did better when girls were around. It was called showing off. And now that the girls we sat next to every day in class were coming out to watch us play and cheer us on, we were motivated to improve our play just enough to be better than we thought we were. It's one thing to be up at the plate when all in the game—both teammates and opponents alike—are totally consumed by the tension, and concentrating on the play. It's quite another to be in the exact same situation with Eleanor Johnson, about whom I could not stop thinking, standing there urging me on to get a hit. Somehow, at that point in life, it was important to figure out how not to disappoint her.

We were also doing what good teams do—winning close games. If you look at the history of championship teams—in any sport—you'll see that they win more games by one run, basket, or goal than they do by smashing their opponents every time out. Championship teams are what they are because they meet the challenge of the *psychological* aspects of competing; they succeed *despite* the anxiety, the pressure, the idea that one mistake at the wrong time could cost the team the game. I had seen players on major league teams make such mistakes, had made them myself, and by this point in my own career as a ball player I was experienced enough to know what to say or do to guide us through potentially rough moments. We began to believe in ourselves, and our winning record propelled us into the 7A championship game against 7A-4, our friendly rivals who were the second-smartest section in the 7A group.

At this point, as it does in every sport at every level, fate intervened. We lost the services of our star first baseman, Harry Barnett, who was home with the flu, and I was faced with the task of going into the championship game against our healthy opponents seriously undermanned. The day before the game Mr. Dickstein, our adviser, asked me to stand up before the class and rally the troops, both the players and our distaff supporters. I began to talk about how great a season we had had, how hard we had worked, how much fun we had experienced, and how personally satisfying it had been for me to get the team to this point. I was preparing the class for the inevitable—that without the services of young, strapping Harry we were going to lose. I could see the look of hurt and disappointment in the faces of my twelve-year-old classmates, especially the girls. It was a shock to them to hear me talk like this, but in my mind I was only being candid and realistic. There was no point in pretending that we had a chance. Although many players on the team had contributed during the season, Harry was our only real star, and his absence in my mind had already sealed our fate.

But Mr. Dickstein had heard enough. In gentle, corrective tones, he interrupted me in mid-sentence to say that I had no way of knowing what the final outcome of the game would be, that we had shown both ourselves and the school that we knew how to win, and that, although Harry's absence was a blow to our chances, it was inappropriate of me to give up before the contest, that any of us had the potential to rise to the occasion and lead the team to victory. He told me that my responsibility as the manager was to believe in the team, to keep the faith as it were, and that the outcome would be what it would be. Don't accept defeat, he said, before you play the contest.

When 7A-4 saw us in the school yard, their first question was "Where's Harry?" When they learned that we would be playing without him in the lineup, they jumped up and down and taunted us, saying that we had no chance, that we might as well forfeit before the game because it wasn't even going to be close. We huddled near our bench, put our hands together, and vowed to give it our best.

I think 7A-4 was looking for a quick knockout, and when that failed to materialize, it took the mettle out of them. Harry's replacement was outstanding both in hitting and in the field, and the tense game went into the eighth tied at 3. We pushed across a run in that inning to go ahead 4–3, and went into the ninth needing three outs to be the champs of 7A. They got a runner on second with two outs, with their best hitter at the plate. My heart was beating so fast and so loud I could have been a conga drum. The girls were screaming. Spectators ringed the school yard, and all I could think about was one more out.

Their guy hit a sharp grounder to me at third base. As I saw the ball coming, I could at the same time feel my body get even tenser, and also filter out everything and focus on the bouncing, blurry white sphere. I was in what athletes call the zone. For the first time in my life I was out of body, and everything seemed to be moving in slow motion. I fielded the ball cleanly, threw over to first for the final out, and for the first time ever I was experiencing the feeling of being a champion.

We screamed and hugged, then went slack and tumbled

to the ground. But I must confess that the best feeling came when I looked over at the stunned, slack-jawed silent expressions of our opponents. They had belittled us, verbally trashed us, dismissed us as frauds, and here we were, in a word, gloating over their defeated countenances. But then my mood changed, and somehow all I could think about was how disappointed, how demoralized they were feeling. I led the team over to them to utter the mandatory "Good game, tough game" valedictories. There would be plenty of time to celebrate out of sight of 7A-4.

Well, the geeks, nerds, and bookworms of 7A-2 had done it. We were the champs of our grade, but of course Americans love only the winner of winners, and now our task was an even more daunting one. We next had to play the winners of the 7B sections—7B-1. These guys were bigger, older, cockier, and more experienced, and since 7B-1 was in the middling range as far as the tracking system was concerned, there were kids in the section who had been for one reason or another forced to repeat grades, and so 7B-1 had *thirteen*-year olds in their section. And to add to the virtual impossibility of our team being able to remain on the same field with our opponents, these guys were so good that they had already beaten the winner of the *8A* sections. The contest was like asking the Vienna Boys Choir to play the Harlem Globetrotters in basketball. We were there because someone had to be, sacrificial lambs, and no one in the school thought we had a chance.

But we went about preparing ourselves for the game in our usual way—we focused on playing at the best of our capabilities—and with Harry Barnett back in the lineup with a serious look on his face, we knew we did have a chance. If we played our game—good fielding, clutch hitting, taking advantage of our opportunities and the inevitable mistakes made by the other team—we would at least be competitive.

And of course everything had changed as a result of our victory the week before over 7A-4. Success is infectious. Once you have experienced it, once you have declared a goal in life—any goal—and have achieved it, it automatically reprograms a part of your brain—the part that deals with your ability to succeed in the future—and somehow tells you that whatever you did not only can be duplicated, it can be surpassed. A copy of your success is imprinted, lodged in just the right spot, and it not only gives you the confidence to succeed again, it propels you toward that success.

And so while I wasn't certain of victory, I thought it was a possibility. I could even detect the slightest sign of doubt in the mien of Mr. Dickstein, who, while he was not one to throw in the towel before the contest, was nevertheless not one to bet on a lost cause either. He looked at our opponents, the conquerors of a section a half-grade older then they, and he looked at us, barely out of *elementary* school, and I'm sure he saw the handwriting on the wall.

But the game still had to be played. This time the crowd that had assembled to watch us was even larger than before, as everyone was there to witness the inevitable slaughter that was about to take place. 7B-1 jumped out to an early lead, scoring two runs in the first, but couldn't put us away early. We settled down and cut the lead to one by the fifth inning and were now in sync—not making any errors, getting guys

on base—and our spirits were up since we hadn't fallen behind by six or seven runs. We felt we still had a chance, and
we could see that our opponents were incredulous that they
had not already sealed the outcome. They began to physically
intimidate us, knocking us over in the field and on the base-
paths, and the sponsor of the games, Mr. Cannon, a history
teacher, had to warn them on more than one occasion that he
would forfeit the game to us if they didn't stop. They toned
down their antics, but it didn't prevent them from playing a
very rough game. If a fight were to break out, I knew that the
only player on our side who could stand up to these guys was
Harry, and I wasn't sure he'd be into it. But we talked when it
was our turn to bat about how we could use their obvious
shock at our competitiveness to our advantage. Let's not try to
kill the ball, which they were trying to do repeatedly, only to
be called out time and again by Mr. Cannon for hitting above
the knees. Let's just try to place our hits between the infield-
ers, and if we held them, which we were doing with their
help, we could push across a few runs and win the game.

This was even better than the majors. The girls in our section were apoplectic with excitement. The little runts of 7A-2
were just a few innings and a few runs away from playing for
the championship of the entire school, and now the spectators
were beginning to root for us in a vociferous manner.

Good sports teams not only know how to win close games,
they know how to come from behind to win late in games as
well. With our team still down by one run going into the eighth,
I hit a single, which was followed by Peter Goodman's single.
This brought up Harry, who I could tell was intent on hitting

the ball down the throats of our misbehaving opponents. He smacked a hard triple into the outfield, scoring Peter and me, and even though we couldn't bring him home to give us an insurance run, we still went into the ninth ahead 3–2.

But 7B-1 still didn't get it. Blinded by their shock, their embarrassment, their inability to pulverize us, they were locked into the mind-set of trying to win the game with one hard swing. Their first two players were called out for hitting above the knees, and when their third man grounded weakly to second base, David had conquered Goliath. We had done it again. Against the odds, we had won.

We had to leave the field quickly, as our vanquished opponents began to make threatening gestures, but Mr. Cannon judiciously intervened and calmed everyone down. They reluctantly congratulated us as we did a little taunting ourselves. This had been a tough, physical, emotional experience. They had made it very difficult for us to concentrate on playing, as the threat of physical violence seemed to be perpetually lurking in the background. But still we had prevailed, and I was feeling the power that comes with achievement, with knowing that one is good at what one does, that in the arena of competition one can excel. This, my first foray into organized competitive sports, was proving to be a training ground in which all my future successes in life would be rooted. A team of which I was part, *of which I was the manager,* was succeeding beyond all expectations, and my ability to understand what that success was based on—focus, teamwork, desire, keeping within one's limits, never giving up, and finally, believing that success was possible—gave me the confidence later in life to take risks, to reach beyond my comfort zone and do things I hadn't done before.

One team now stood between 7A-2 and the championship of Jay Cooke Junior High School—8B-2. They had already defeated 9B-3, the victors of the ninth-grade title game, and these guys were not only even bigger, faster, stronger, and more sure of themselves than any team we had played so far, they had beaten every one of their opponents decisively. There had been no squeakers, no one-run games in their record. They had blown through the opposition without ever being tested. They were so confident of defeating us that in the days preceding the game, during our frequent encounters in the hallways, they would put their arms around us, these guys who were four, five, six inches taller and up to fifty pounds heavier than we were, and jokingly say that they would go easy on us, that they would keep their run total under fifty.

By this time, I had enough confidence in myself and in our team that, again, I thought we could win if—as we had done before—we could keep the score close early in the game. We had cleverly used the element of surprise to our advantage, the surprise that we were still competitive into the middle innings. This had totally demoralized our opponents and enabled us to keep the games close enough to then win late. Although it was hard to pin our hopes on such a tenuous strategy, I knew there was no way we could dominate them. We scored our runs in ones and twos, they scored theirs in bunches.

We hit first and went down one-two-three before taking the field, confidently looking forward to being the champions of the school in an hour or so. I had no way of knowing that the game would be over in a matter of minutes. I had never in all the years of playing boxball seen such power, such skill, such ability. They were awesome. The score was 6–0 after one inning, and it only got worse after that. They hit balls that left the infield so fast—*without flying above the knees*—that we had no chance to react to them, let alone field them cleanly to try to throw the runners out. Doubles, triples, and home runs—too numerous to count—rang out through the school yard, and I have a very vivid picture in my mind, even to this day, of standing at my position at third base and watching our out-fielders chase their smashes into the nether reaches of the yard.

By the third inning, my disappointment had turned into mirthful resignation, as they had already pushed across sixteen runs. We finally scored our first and second runs after that, when they generously and deliberately—patronizingly, some would say—mishandled our hits, and suddenly the kids of 7A-2 were exposed for what we were—a Cinderella team whose clock had finally struck midnight. We had reached the limit of our ability. The final score was 32–3, and it wasn't even that close. They could have scored 75 times had they wanted, but they let up because everyone wanted to see the debacle end.

The girls cried, we consoled ourselves while laughing at the enormity of the mismatch, and the next day Mr. Dickstein told us in front of the class how proud he was at our accomplishments, that we had gone way beyond our potential and had nothing to be ashamed of or embarrassed about. I heard his words and understood their meaning, but it was still difficult for me to accept what had happened, although I think it would have been worse had the game been close and had they scored two runs in the bottom of the ninth to beat us 5–4.

Defeat is as great a teacher as victory, even more so in many ways. In victory there is a tendency to overlook one's weaknesses, to focus only on what's working to bring about, rather than undermine, the desired result. In defeat, weaknesses are glaring. But defeat is also a part of success—even great teams are rarely undefeated—and it is in agony, in seeing one's will stymied, that the seeds of future success are planted. I don't think there was anything I could have done differently that day as the manager of my team to defeat the behemoths of 8B-2. We were just overmatched physically. But just being on the same field with them, just remembering after all these years what is was like to experience the thrill of competing for the championship when all that mattered to me was sports, provided me with a preview of what life is like when it is lived well.

In a fortune cookie a few years back I found the saying "Great things are made of little things." Nothing could better describe success in life—or in sports. When it comes to playing ball, this is the way the game must be played to be effective. Winning at baseball is a matter of doing the little things that lead to winning play—catching the ball when it is hit to you, making accurate throws to your teammates, moving the runner along so that a hit by someone else might score him, throwing strikes as a pitcher so that the opposing team earns its base runners rather than being granted them through bases on balls. There is an infinite number of plays that are made every time two teams square off against each other, and the athletes that make them more often usually play for successful teams.

But winning is not the only reward in competition, perhaps not even the most important one. And certainly winning does not result merely from an obsessive desire to win. The rewards of competition are more personal. They help us to develop, to see how skillful we are at handling different circumstances, to rebound from defeat, to enjoy victory magnanimously, without gloating, to witness the fruits of our labor through dedication and practice, to set a goal and to work steadily at it, to share our successes with others. All these things are the little things that the fortune was alluding to, and they apply to all areas of life, to the learning of a new language as much as the mastering of a musical instrument.

As modern living becomes more complex by the day, I have found that the simple truths are the most helpful, and simply paying attention is one of them. Succeeding in life for me at this point is a matter of running hard to first base when I hit a grounder, keeping my eye on the ball when I'm batting, and never, ever letting the score dictate how I feel about the contest. Whether I am ahead or behind is of little concern to me. I have learned to detach the effort from the result. Of the former I am in complete control. The latter is governed by forces I cannot control, and learning to accept that fact is something I am continuing to incorporate into every fiber of my being.

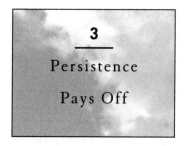

3

Persistence

Pays Off

BY THE 1963 football season, the Philadel-
phia Eagles had fallen from the lofty perches of their 1960
championship victory over the legendary Green Bay Packers
of Vince Lombardi, and were a dreadful team, but that didn't
stop me and my best friend Peter Goodman from becoming
season ticket holders. On seven Sunday afternoons during that
long and losing autumn, we made our way to Franklin Field
on the campus of the University of Pennsylvania to sit packed
like sardines in our $3 end-zone seats and watch the Birds get
beaten by almost every one of their opponents.

My disappointment at seeing the team I rooted for lose
week after week was mitigated somewhat by a ritual that
Peter and I carried out after each game. Although the contests
were televised back to the cities from which the visiting teams
hailed, they were played in an era before television dominated
sports. There wasn't the array of reporters, producers, and as-
sorted technicians that is now a permanent feature of the sports

landscape. So when my buddy and I made a beeline for the spot where the athletes emerged from their locker rooms to board buses that would whisk them off to hotels or airports or other parts unknown to us, it was actually easy to get right next to them and ask for their autographs, which we did every week. This was also in the days before the autographs of sports figures became commodities to be bought, sold, and traded on the open market. Since it was unheard of for a player to expect payment for the illegible chicken scratch that passed as his signature, as the season progressed Peter and I filled page after page of the small autograph books that were then in vogue among schoolchildren.

The procedure for securing the signatures was quite simple. We had plenty of time to get to the door before they did, and so we just waited around until they started to come out. Since we also collected football cards, we pretty much could connect the faces to the names, and since we had already managed to obtain the signatures of the Eagles, by mid-season we had begun to concentrate on those of their opponents, of the Redskins, Giants, Cardinals, Bears, and other teams that came into Franklin Field, defeated the Eagles, and left for the following week's assignment.

The reason why autographs were so important to me at the time can be explained by understanding why anyone covets something that is connected to his or her hero. To admire or revel in the existence of someone famous—either a rock star, politician, athlete, or actor—is to proclaim to the world that one wants to identify with that person, to be touched personally by his or her existence, to bathe in the light of reflected glory. I wanted to believe that what I was looking at down there on the field and on television was what I aspired to be as an athlete. Until I began to develop a sense of the complexity of life, sports was it. For me and for many other young men in America at that time, sports was the *only* way a male could test his strength, his agility, his speed, his coordination, his stamina, and his toughness—all the qualities that society proclaimed a man should possess to succeed as an adult—and I had bought into the enculturation from the start. The only other avenue to success for a boy was to be smart in school, but that route had a double edge, for even though it was encouraged by the mostly female elementary school teachers, in some male quarters it was considered sissified to be too smart and studious. But excelling on the diamond, the field, or the court prompted unmitigated approval from one's peers. There was no greater sense of achievement, no more exacting set of standards, than to play sports well, and so the ballplayers were considered the real men of society, the ones whom young boys wanted to emulate, and their autographs were a way to get closer to these almost mythical figures, to develop relationships with them, to interact and feel the power of their presence.

My earliest fantasies, the first books I read, and many of the discussions that were held in a household that included three males, and an extended family that contained many more, were about sports. I grew up steeped in this tradition, and even now, as an adult, although my interest is not nearly as intense as it was back then, I cannot go more than a day or two without having to know what took place in whatever professional sport is in season, even if I spend only five minutes finding out. It is as if I am addicted to a long-running soap opera that plays day after day, year after year; as in daytime television, the faces may change, and the particular situation may be different—from episode to episode, season to season— but the basic story line remains the same. I still derive a certain vicarious pleasure knowing that what these men do with their bodies as professionals, how they call upon their muscles, tendons, and bones to perform outrageous feats of physical strength, speed, and agility, is what I aspired to do at one point in my life, and that memory has stayed with me.

On one particular Sunday halfway through that sad and disappointing season, the Cleveland Browns were in town, and that meant that I would have the opportunity to obtain the John Hancock of the star of stars, the best player in the game—the great runner Jim Brown. To no one's surprise, the Browns ripped right through the Eagles, and Jim Brown had one of the best days of his career. As the game wore on, all I could think of was getting down to the street after the game to be in a position to get his autograph.

Jim Brown was notoriously sullen, grim, and moody. He never seemed to smile. He had a totally intimidating bearing both on and off the field, but I had set my mind to the task of getting his autograph, and whether I got it or not, I was at least going to try as hard as I could. While most players would scribble something on their way to the team bus without much fanfare or resistance, Jim Brown was not known to give autographs. My goal would be challenging, and throughout the second half of the game I was mentally preparing myself for the work that lay ahead. My plan was to totally focus on him, and not be diverted by other autograph possibilities.

Brown's signature on the field was, after being tackled, to get up very slowly and walk back equally slowly to the huddle. It was become increasingly clear as we waited in the brisk autumn air with darkness beginning to enfold us that he was equally slow in getting out of the locker room. Dozens of players were passing right by but I kept my eyes riveted on the door, waiting for arguably the best player ever to play the game. Jim Brown's skills were so superior that it was only in the 1994 season, nearly thirty years after his sudden and un-expected retirement, that his record for scoring the most touchdowns in an NFL career was broken by the 49ers great receiver, Jerry Rice.

At a certain point, the crowd of autograph seekers wait-ing for the great player to appear began to doubt that he would come out at all. Most of the players had gone by and boarded one of the buses that was perhaps fifty yards from where we stood, and a rumor began to circulate that he had gone out through another door and slipped by us unnoticed. When even more time passed without sight of him, some of the crowd began to leave in disappointment. But not me. I was fourteen years old, had no other place to be, and until I saw with my own eyes the two buses—with their motors running at the curb—pull away, I wasn't moving.

No player had appeared for ten minutes, and although one bus had already driven off, the other one was still idling, and now the crowd was perhaps half the size it had been fif-teen minutes earlier. It was now cold and almost dark, and thoughts of getting back on the subway to make the hour-ride home were beginning to creep into my determined brain. And then, like Moses coming down from the mountain, he was there. The door opened and through it slowly walked this large, handsome, scowling man, who could not be anyone but Jim Brown.

He pulled the group of people, now numbering perhaps twelve, to him like a magnet, making it difficult to navigate his way to the bus. After carrying the football twenty-five or thirty times that afternoon, and getting knocked to the hard ground nearly every time, he was obviously sore, and he was in no hurry to get to the bus, taking one slow step after the other.

But neither was he signing any autographs, and he seemed totally impervious to the imprecations of the crowd of seekers that had attached itself to him, pens in hands, begging with him, pleading with him, to sign their books and programs.

"Here, Mr. Brown."

"Please, Mr. Brown."

"Hey, Jim, would you sign this for me?"

"It's for my daughter, Mr. Brown."

"Great game, Jim, how about an autograph?"

"Mr. Brown, Mr. Brown."

"Mr. Brown."

"MR. BROWN."

"MR. BROWN!!!"

He had made it—along with his impromptu entourage—halfway to the bus, and not only had he not shown the slightest inclination to sign his name, he had not even acknowledged the presence of any of us. Since he was taller than the increasingly forlorn individuals who were shoving books, papers, and pens up at his face, he just looked straight ahead at how much farther he had to go to reach the bus and be rid of this clinging knot of irritants.

By this point I knew that my dreams of getting his autograph were about to be dashed if I didn't do something fast. I began to worm my way through the crowd toward him, using my size (I was about 5'3" at that time) to my advantage. Somehow I got up close and was standing directly in front of him as he slowly, inexorably made his way to the still-idling bus. But unlike the other seekers, who walked along looking in the same direction as the star, I faced him and was walking backward as he made his way through the crowd.

Something about my moxie must have touched him; when he for the first time on this protracted journey looked down and saw my visage gazing up at him, arms uplifted, eyes riveted on his, he uttered the only words I or anyone else in that group heard him say that day. Looking directly at me, without so much as a hint of a smile, he said, "What are you doin', blockin' for me?" Although it wasn't much, nevertheless I had gotten through his impassive, intimidating demeanor. I had made a connection.

In the next moments I felt as if I were on the field. My attention was totally focused on him, and I blotted out everyone and everything else. I began to ask him over and over again, almost in a whisper, for his autograph, and although from time to time during the next two or three minutes he looked down to see if he still had his blocker, and even once let one corner of his mouth move up in the faintest, most ironic smile I had ever seen, he never once made a move to sign either mine or anyone else's book. By this time I had put any thought about whether I was going to get or not get his autograph out of my mind. I didn't know whether I would get it, or even cared if I got it, all I knew is that I had to keep my eye on the ball, and that meant not losing my position in front of Jim Brown as his interference. I wanted him to reward me, and so I stood my ground. I made sure I kept even pace with him, so that he had enough room to walk, but not so much that someone could slip between us. Something made me think that if anyone were to succeed in obtaining his signature, it would be me, but he never showed any inclination at all that he was going to stop his march and scribble his name.

There is something mystical about being caught up in a drama that transcends the mere details of events themselves and becomes some other kind of human interaction. If a creature from another planet, or another time on earth perhaps, had witnessed this spectacle, he would have found it totally impossible to understand. The energy inside the cluster was completely self-contained—unlike anything on the outside. We were close. We were tight. We were locked in a kind of dance that saw me try to wear down his resistance with cuteness, boldness, seductiveness, or with anything I could come up with. And he was just as determined to be who he was at that moment, and that clearly meant that he was not going to sign any autographs, not for his blocker, nor for anyone else.

We were now no more than ten yards from the bus, and

the great Jim Brown was just seconds away from holding on to his obvious resolve to not be an ingratiating sports star. He had not been mean, nasty, or threatening, he just had never made the slightest gesture of compliance with the requests of the individuals who were now no more than an accompaniment to the team bus. As soon as he reached the door, the crowd parted in front of him, like the waters of the Red Sea as the Hebrews fled from Pharaoh. One by one the disappointed autograph-seekers began to peel away from the crowd and turn their thoughts to what they were going to eat for dinner. They had given their best effort and, since they could not very well follow him onto the team bus, had failed in their mission. But they could at least assure themselves that they had done all they could.

I must confess that I *thought* about following him onto the bus, but there were lengths to which even I would not go, and that was one of them. But neither had I given up, and suddenly I saw an opening that might be one last slight opportunity before Jim Brown would move off into the night.

As he stepped onto the bus to take his seat, he was forced to walk down the center aisle to a spot at the rear because most of the seats in the front were occupied. I walked alongside him as he slowly made his way back—even though he was in the bus and of course I was on the street outside. If he decided to turn right and sit on the side of the bus away from the curb, my quest was over, since the street was moderately trafficked, and it would have been dangerous to venture out to where he was sitting. But he turned left instead, and plunked himself down next to the window about three rows before the very back of the bus. I was still in the game.

By this time, there were two or three other people keeping pace with me, although since I clearly had a plan and they did not, they had to remain a few paces behind to see what I was going to do next. I stood right outside his seat and held up my book. If he opened the window, I would be able to reach up and get the autograph I had been focusing on all afternoon, especially for the past twenty minutes. But he was in no mood to relent, and for about a minute I just stood there, waiting in vain for something to happen, for him to reward my patience and persistence with what he knew I wanted more than anything in the world. But he remained steadfast. There were on this day to be no autographs.

It was at that point that he made a mistake, or rather he made a move that turned out to be a mistake simply because our game was on my turf and I knew the terrain better than he did. He needed air. The bus must have been hot, he had spent the afternoon in the most extreme kind of physical exertion, and the last few minutes had not been easy either. He did what any other person would have done in that situation—he opened the window about an inch.

There wasn't enough room to thrust my hands and book up into his face, but I knew something about the windows on these buses that he didn't. After all, as a fourteen-year-old without a driver's license, these vehicles were *my* form of transportation. I practically lived on these buses, and so in a way I suddenly had an unfair advantage, which I immediately seized.

There were flanges on both sides of the windows that had to be squeezed in order to raise the window from the closed position and then to lower it completely, but once the window was open—even slightly—it wasn't necessary to squeeze the flanges to widen the opening. And in that moment on the street, I knew I was faced with the most difficult decision of the afternoon. The bus was moments from pulling away, so I didn't have much time. I had to decide. Should I put my hand under the window and lift it from the outside, or should I continue to plead from the street? That was the choice I faced. If I continued with the strategy I had employed till that point, it was very unlikely that I would succeed. But if I opened the window, I was taking another risk. I was transgressing the boundary of his space. Although he was on the inside and I on the outside, I was putting myself on a limb as soon as my hand crossed the plane of the bus. He would have had every right to be angry at my insolence, and of course there was no guarantee if I did decide to trespass that he would sign his name.

But we were playing a game, and when I play I play to win. I counted on the fact that my youth and my size were going to keep me from getting hurt, and that the worst that could happen was that I'd be warned or scolded, and I would go home without Jim Brown's autograph. I could live with that.

I felt a surge of exhilaration as all in one motion I placed my left hand firmly under the window, lifted it, and extended my right hand with my book and my pen up and into the dark, mysterious bus. I looked at him. He looked right back at me. I said, "Please, Mr. Brown," as his entire face registered incredulity at the *chutzpah* this pint-sized teenager was demonstrating. I'm sure that had he given himself a moment to think about what was happening, he might have considered shutting the window on my hand, but perhaps he also felt that somehow in the cosmic order of things I deserved to get what I had so doggedly sought. He took my pen, scribbled something in my book, and handed them back to me.

As I pulled my arms out of the bus, the window shut tightly and moments later the vehicle pulled away from the curb. I looked down to see the plainly legible name of Jim Brown written in the center of the page. Victory!

Something had propelled me forward that day. Perhaps there is something wise about New Yorkers and other city dwellers not wanting to make eye contact with strangers, because doing so establishes a relationship that always has the potential of leading to something one cannot control or that might even become dangerous. As far as I was concerned, when Jim Brown spoke to me, engaged me even for an instant, from that point on I felt entitled to take liberties, to allow the personal contact we had to dictate my strategy. When he talked to me, he knew me. I knew him. And his successful attempt to distance himself from the crowd did not take into account that he had given me an emotional opening that would later become an actual, spatial opening.

Of course on another level I was flirting with danger by lifting the window, but at no time did I *sense* that anything harmful would befall me. At worst I was a pest, and he treated me that way—as he had treated the others—by ignoring my request. But when I had the audacity to violate the sanctity of the team bus for the sake of his signature, there was some part of him that resonated with what I had done, that wanted to reward my cleverness and my persistence, that was inclined to reinforce in this budding young adult the notion that exerting oneself, that taking the extra step, is often what separates those who get what they want from those who don't, which is of course the very way he ran with the football.

And I like to think that the reason why the window slammed shut after he had signed my book—which I still have—was not out of disgust for what had just transpired but because to his way of thinking I was the only one of the seekers who deserved to have his prayers answered, and not only because of those prayers, but because I had the courage and the faith to act upon them. My father always says that God helps those who help themselves.

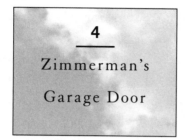

4

Zimmerman's

Garage Door

I SPENT MY teen years in the suburbs, which to me meant one thing—isolation. Shortly after my Bar Mitzvah, my parents heeded the siren call of Newer, Cleaner, and More Modern, and moved to a remote area of Philadelphia that consisted of tracts of black-and-white split-level homes, all looking pretty much the same, even if the den was on the left side in some of the houses, on the right in others. Our new neighborhood was in sharp contrast to the one in which I had spent my early years, where small stores and grocery markets peppered virtually every corner. That was a community in which the merchants kept a record of how much you owed them on 3-by-5 cards, doctors still made house calls, and a public school was so close I could walk to it without adult supervision from the first grade on.

Our new neighborhood was predicated on the great social invention of the twentieth century—the automobile. We had just one bus line, which ran mostly during morning and evening rush hours, infrequently on Saturdays, and not at all on Sundays. Anyone living in the neighborhood who did not have a car was simply not in control of his or her life—and that meant me, because it would be three years before I reached the legal driving age. Since my parents worked mostly evenings and weekends—the times when I was not in school—I was at the mercy of the W bus line, which took me to and from high school, an hour's ride each way, but did nothing to satisfy my adolescent weekend wanderlust.

I managed to grudgingly tolerate my predicament, given that I really had no choice, but what I spent a lot of my free time doing was dreaming about being behind the wheel and zooming off wherever and whenever I wanted. In my fantasies I was free, never having to plan my outings with the almost-never-to-be-seen W bus in mind.

My desire to slide into the driver's seat and take off in our blue '60 Dodge Dart with push-button transmission reached almost obsessive dimensions, especially after my father sat me on his lap and let me drive in a small circle on an empty parking lot one afternoon shortly after we moved. I would spend long periods of time just sitting in the car. Hour after hour would go by and I would still be there. Every so often I would place my hands on the wheel, look in the rear- and side-view mirrors, put my foot on the brake and gas pedals, and pretend to drive. My imagination took me to various places—strolling on the boardwalk in Atlantic City, New Jersey, pulling up to the Holland Tunnel to enter the exotic terrain of New York City, or cruising the Pennsylvania Dutch country not far from where we lived.

My imagination would often include a female companion, as often as not a girl named Donna, sitting next to me, my right elbow resting comfortably on the back of the car seat, my hand on her shoulder. I could easily turn the wheel with my free left arm—in fact I could do it with the heel of my hand—and my girlfriend would see in me a reflection of my driving technique: a man with power. Her freedom would be in my hands, and just thinking about this possibility enabled me to feel more alive as I sat whiling away hours in my parents' car in front of our house, my sixteenth birthday eighteen, eleven, eight, or five months in the future.

But time does pass, even at an age when it seems that the things one wants the most take the longest to arrive, and soon I found myself enrolled in a driver's training school, operated by a friend of the family, far from us on the other side of town. Every Tuesday and Thursday after school I would take public transportation—a bus and an elevated train—to learn the skills that would provide me with my coveted ticket to freedom. When I finally held my learner's permit in my hands, with the official seal of the Commonwealth of Pennsylvania stamped on it, I knew there was a God.

My lessons got off to a shaky start. I found it surprisingly difficult to get into the rhythm of driving. On one occasion, while making a right—not the most difficult of maneuvers— the car suddenly stopped halfway through the turn. My teacher had engaged the brake on his side to avoid hitting a parked car.

Perhaps I was tired from having spent a long day at school, and then having to trek for an hour to my lessons, but the early prognosis was not good. Reports were beginning to filter back to my folks that I wasn't making much progress, and I began to fear that my hopes for life on the road would be dashed. Worst of all would be the embarrassment of not being able to learn how to drive, when my classmates, one by one, were acquiring their licenses.

But hearing that my driving habits were erratic challenged me to do better, and soon I realized that what I really lacked above all was focus. I was too concerned with the *rewards* of the process, and not concerned enough with the process itself—the mechanics of learning a skill that would provide me with what I desired. As so often happened in my early life, the bad report card spurred me to concentrate on the task at hand. My studies improved immediately, and before long my instructor felt I was ready to take the test.

I could not sleep for days. Although failure to pass the exam would not preclude the possibility of taking it again, I would still be forced to deal with the ignominy of not having passed the first time, something my classmates would never have let me live down. And of course it was so important for me to succeed right away because I had fantasized about driving for years, and I could not bear the thought of enduring one more day without a license.

My father drove me to the testing site, and before long I was seated next to a stern, no-nonsense state trooper right out of central casting, who gave me clear instructions as he got into the car. Soon I was out on the course and I knew immediately that I would make the grade. I felt confident, secure, at ease, certain of how to manage behind the wheel. At one point, as I began to imagine myself out on the open road, I entered a kind of reverie that put my driving on automatic. I was so transported, knowing for certain that I would pass the exam, that I barely noticed my father waiting at the end of the course, discreetly but firmly moving his palms down over and over in a gesture that clearly meant "Slow down!" I did, and received my passing grade from the suddenly friendly officer.

Nirvana! Not only had I achieved a certain rank in life, I had passed the exam with ease. I was now the newest member of The Holy Order of Drivers, and was poised to enter a world about which I had only dreamed. Gone were the days and nights of isolation and hopelessness; gone was the feeling of being stuck in a sterile, monotonous world that afforded me little opportunity for exploration. Arrived was the sweet aroma of possibility, the fragrance of which would waft through the nostrils of my teenaged nose whenever I placed the key in the ignition.

There was one minor problem. I had no car. We were at this point a one-vehicle family, and that one vehicle and I were rarely at home at the same time. Although I could gaze contentedly at the card in my wallet that proved I was able to drive without an accompanying adult, that didn't get me anywhere as far as I was concerned. I was still grounded, and my impatience mounted as my parents debated their options. They could see how eager I was to set sail for parts unknown, and, being accommodating, reasonable people, they were inclined to grant my request for some sort of vehicle to satisfy the demands my adolescent hormones were making. They decided to buy a new car and allow me to drive the soon-to-be-old one. But the gray '65 Pontiac Catalina with the black vinyl top had to be ordered. It would take eight weeks and, in the meantime, the W bus and I were still fated to be best friends.

Weeks had gone by since the day I passed my exam and still I had never driven. I wasn't practicing, wasn't developing confidence, wasn't out there on the highways and byways with the push-button transmission. I was sulking, brooding, complaining, railing against my circumstances, each day not behind the wheel only deepening my despair.

And then there was a breakthrough. On Easter Sunday, 1965, my parents were off from work, which meant that their car was available to me. I jumped at the chance, making plans to visit a friend—Stuart Zimmerman—who lived a half hour from my house. I called and made arrangements to pick up two other friends—Joe Gold and Carl Wolf—along the way.

I did not get off to a particularly good start. My father asked me to back the Dodge onto our driveway so that he could remove a few things from the trunk, and somehow the left side of the car ended up on the lawn. Dad shook his head in resignation, wondering no doubt if he had made the right decision to allow me to drive off in the vehicle he used for work. Was I ready? Could I handle it? Was he still going to have a car in one piece that ran at the end of the day?

He crossed his fingers and offered last-minute instructions. As I pulled away, all I could think of was the fact that Liberation Day had finally arrived. Hot damn! I was gone. I was free. I was a sixteen-year-old boy with a driver's license *and* a vehicle, and nothing in the world was going to stop me. It was show time!

I picked up Carl and Gold and we made it to Zimmerman's house without difficulty. Traffic was light and we spent a long afternoon messing around, listening to the Beatles' *Rubber Soul*, Bob Dylan, and a lot of Temptations, talking about school and girls, eating hoagie sandwiches and drinking Mountain Dew. I was on Cloud Nine. I couldn't believe this day had finally arrived. I was sharing my triumph with a few of my buddies and with the car that was soon to be mine to drive, which the guys immediately and fittingly dubbed the Epmobile.

The hours passed and when it was time to leave, Gold, Carl, and I left by the back door to drive home. The car was parked in the driveway, which sloped down at a fairly steep angle to the garage door. When I had initially pulled in, I had gone a bit too far and now found myself a little closer to the door than I wanted to be, perhaps two feet away. The task I had before me was to back out quickly enough to avoid going forward—something the car would undoubtedly do if there wasn't enough initial speed to overcome the incline.

No problem. Piece of cake. We discussed my options for about five minutes and agreed, although Carl and Joe didn't drive yet, that the best move would be to hit the gas pedal hard before removing the parking brake. That way as soon as the brake was released, there would already be enough power to move the car back without rolling ahead. It was a good plan. We piled in and I—my glands pumping out so much adrenaline that I could hardly maintain control over basic motor functions—turned on the ignition.

The plan would work, I said to myself over and over. My

hands were shaking as I grabbed the steering wheel and put my right foot down hard on the gas pedal. The engine revved up loudly as I quickly released the parking brake, put my right arm over the back of the seat, and turned around to guide the car smoothly and rapidly in reverse.

It would be hard for anyone to imagine my utter horror as a few seconds later the front of the Epmobile had come to rest three feet into the Zimmermans' garage door. I had been so focused on getting enough power to back up that I had neglected one small detail—pushing the reverse button on the transmission. The car, still in neutral, had rolled forward when I released the brake and crashed through the bottom half of the door. The sound of crunching wood on this otherwise calm and quiet Easter Sunday was loud enough to have been heard across the Delaware River in New Jersey.

My sweet dreams of freedom shattered along with the door, I immediately entered the Twilight Zone. I didn't think it was possible, but the adrenaline rush was even greater than before. With neither the experience nor the maturity to cope with such a blunder, I could think of nothing but escape. If we could only get out of there fast enough, perhaps no one would know what had happened. Maybe, just maybe, I could get away with this, and not have to face the consequences of my ineptitude.

I pushed reverse and backed out of the shattered door so fast that I failed to see a metal clothesline pole that stood at the top of the driveway. I went straight into it, bending it in half. I popped the transmission into drive and sped off, barely able to

maintain my composure. There wasn't a doubt in the world—
my driving debut was a flop.

Carl and Joe sat utterly silent as I went over and over in
my mind about what had just taken place. I was convinced
that the previous five minutes had ruined my life. Although
there had been no damage to the car, which was built like a
tank, Zimmerman's garage door was in pieces. I could think
only of the worst. My father would lose his insurance, I would
be kicked off the coverage, my parents would decide that I
wasn't ready to drive and either cancel the new Pontiac or sell
the Dodge when they did get it, any of which would have the
effect of relegating me back to Suburban Purgatory.

I quickly made up my mind. Since the car didn't even
have a dent, I would keep this little incident to myself. I could
not risk jeopardizing my driving privileges, my future, the
realization of my dreams. My hope was that no one would notice the garage door for a few days, and then, when someone
eventually did, it would be too late to connect me to the scene
of the crime.

I dropped off my accomplices and somehow made my
way back home. I had never been more confused and more
demoralized in my life. I felt like a two-year-old who has colored all over the walls and thinks no one will notice. I couldn't
face my parents because I was not prepared to tell them the
truth. I had not yet learned that life can be forgiving as well as
trying, and that to face one's trials and tribulations with grace-
ful dignity is almost always better than attempting to evade
them. All I could do was say that I had had a great day and

slink off into my room, unable to eat or interact with anyone. Liberation Day had turned into Disaster Day, from which I could not see how to extricate myself. My dilemma was simple—to tell my parents would mean certain grounding, the end of a dream that I had nurtured for three years, and not to tell them was not only wrong, it was stupid. I could see that clearly but I was too overwhelmed by fear and uncertainty to do the right thing.

The next day was even worse. I had to face going back to school to deal with another problem—Zimmerman. If he didn't say anything when I saw him, I would have to continue to pretend that nothing had happened, which would have truly been weird. And if he were to start screaming at me in the middle of the hallway between second and third periods, which was entirely possible, then it would have caused a scene. I decided to take the chicken way out, reflecting my continuing inability to deal with the incident. I pretended to be sick.

I spent the day at home in my pajamas, afflicted with some vague illness that somehow made it difficult for me to go to school. I was barely able to function, obsessed with what had taken place the day before. How could I have been so stupid? It was such a good plan and I had to go and ruin it with a careless mistake, like doing a complicated algebra problem perfectly and then at the very end multiplying 6 times 7 and getting 48. Could I really hope to get away with this? Here it was, Monday afternoon, and still no one apparently knew. How long could I keep this up? Would I go back to school tomorrow? Could I face Zimmerman?

Strangely, I had begun to relax, thinking with each passing hour that I was not going to be called to account for my misdeed, that I would remain despite this incident a child. But then the telephone rang as I picked my way through dinner. My father answered the phone and immediately gave it to me.

"It's for you," he said.

"Who is it?" I asked nervously.

"I don't know," he replied. "A woman."

I knew who it was. "Hello," I said.

"Alan, this is Mrs. Zimmerman." I turned stark white. "You know you drove into my garage door."

"I know."

"Have you told your parents yet?"

"No."

"Don't you think you ought to tell them?"

"Yes."

"Good," she said, "I'll wait to hear from you." The line went dead.

I handed the receiver back to my father and sat there, gazing straight ahead, not knowing what to do. I wanted to say something but all at once the unrelenting stress of the past two days overtook me and I was completely incapable of speech. Nothing I could say would undo what had happened, which is what I truly wanted more than anything else. All this was careening through my mind for what seemed like an eternity when really only a second had elapsed since I had spoken to Mrs. Zimmerman. I could only think of the worst—that I would be forever without wheels.

Then I heard my mother's voice penetrate the trance into

which I had settled. "Did you hit someone with the car?" she said, with a mixture of anxiety and solicitation.

The question—which represented her worst fear—had the immediate effect of breaking the spell, and in that instant I realized that everything was all right, that I had inflated the incident beyond all proportion. I answered no and watched my parents visibly relax. After all, they could see that our car was not bashed or dented, and if I hadn't run anyone over, then they figured that the worst thing that could have happened was that someone else's car was bashed or dented, and that possibility they could handle.

I told them the whole story, detail by agonizing detail. The fact that no one was hurt lightened everyone's mood immeasurably, even made the atmosphere in our kitchen somewhat giddy. How could anyone get upset over a busted garage door, for goodness sakes? My father spared me even further embarrassment and called Mrs. Zimmerman, letting her know that his insurance would cover the cost of the repairs and that I was sorry it had happened. He said that I had made a mistake when I tried to back the car out of the driveway and that I was afraid I wouldn't be able to drive again if I had faced what had happened.

By the time I returned to school the next day—my "illness" having cleared up shortly after Mrs. Zimmerman's phone call—I did have to face reality. Everyone in school knew what had happened. At least they knew the end result rather than the gory details, which I gladly supplied to them free of charge, since by this time the incident had begun to assume mythical proportions in the classrooms, hallways, and ball fields of

Central High School. Zimmerman, who was a good-natured
fellow, brushed it off with a wave of his hand and said it was
no big deal. Carl, Joe, and I got our first big laugh as we went
over the incident, especially the part when I backed up into
the clothesline pole. That was sort of a punctuation mark on
what had turned out to be an all-time adventure.

The destruction of Zimmerman's garage door did not
have an adverse effect on my life. About a month after the incident we did get the Pontiac, enabling me to drive the Epmobile hither and yon. My father said that he suspected I wasn't
quite ready to drive on that Easter Sunday from the rather
"creative" way in which I had backed the car onto the lawn,
but I said that all I needed was practice, and that I would
really learn a lot from what had happened.

And that was certainly the case. I discovered that machines
have a logic of their own, and that the best way to handle them
is to slow down and methodically perform whatever tasks are
necessary to operate them safely and effectively. I found out
that there is usually more time to do whatever I have to do
than I think there is. And I learned that there is a difference
between making a mistake that is really awful and one that is
merely careless and embarrassing, and that part of maturity is
to distinguish one from the other.

I also learned that it's best to try to rectify a mess sooner
rather than later, that disclosing early and completely one's
mistake is better than trying to pretend that nothing happened. This latter route usually ends up producing some kind
of physical symptom that has a much more harmful effect

than taking responsibility for one's actions, which may seem almost impossible to do but which can become habitual, just like anything else. But even if no physical symptoms develop, learning to cope with mistakes is important because every life is full of them, and those who would rather make excuses or blame someone else for something they did are cutting themselves off from opportunities to be courageous—to accept responsibility for one's actions. It is only when one makes a mistake and is forgiven that one learns how to forgive.

But what I discovered above all was that my fear of not getting what I wanted was something I inflated to an unreasonable level. It was I who gave it life. I wanted my freedom so bad that I was blinded to the reality that it was going to take more—much more—than an insignificant mishap to deny the realization of my dream. The incident made me realize that one's mettle will frequently be tested, but that this is the stuff of which life is composed. These events are what gives us character, forms our personalities, and teaches us lessons that could never be taught in school.

Thirty years have gone by since that mild Easter when I feared that the world around me would crash along with Zimmerman's garage door. But the intervening time has given me the opportunity to recognize that no matter how hopeless or terrible I might feel in the midst of a crisis, time will eventually transform what appears to be an impossible situation into one that is merely irritating or entirely manageable, and soon I am wondering—as with the crayons on the wall—what the fuss was all about.

5

The War

at Home

THE MERE MENTION of the word "Vietnam" conjures up many images and emotions to many families, and mine is no exception. Never have I been in a situation where my destiny was linked so dramatically to the life experience of others.

From the beginning of our involvement in that far-off country, my father, after whom I modeled most of my political positions, was anti-war. Even in the mid-sixties, when the United States was becoming more involved in the conflict, he was already saying that the strategy wouldn't work, that we had no real national interest there, that President Johnson couldn't be trusted, and that any attempt to immerse ourselves in a guerrilla war in Southeast Asia would fail. Even when most Americans had no qualms about fighting overseas in a country that very few of us had even heard of, Dad was already voicing his opposition, and it was not difficult for me, as a teenager who admired both my father's thoughtfulness and his serious interest in current events, to adopt his views as my own. Our family had one position when it came to the subject of Vietnam. A sign in our kitchen, where we spent much of our time, read PEACE IS PATRIOTIC.

Thirty years later, I often wonder how much of his opposition was ad hominem. After all, he had two sons, one of whom—me—was in high school, and if this looming catastrophe were to drag on indefinitely, which is precisely what many of the experts he was reading were forecasting, then he would have to face the question of how he would feel about sending me off to fight there. As a veteran of World War II he was certainly no pacifist. But since my mother is a survivor of the Holocaust, and the only other family member to have survived with her was her father, my grandfather, to whom I was very close, it is hardly surprising that my father would have had to evaluate his feelings about which wars were justified, and which were not. Could he truly equate stopping Hitler and his murderous Nazis with dropping napalm on peasants in far-off jungles?

Ultimately, I suspect he was asking himself whether the goals Johnson had set out before the country were worth the possible sacrifice of his two sons. As a father myself of two young boys, I know I would ask that question before unhesitatingly supporting an effort that involved combat. Isn't that the litmus test to which every parent ought to subject himself before supporting a war? In considering our goals in Vietnam, he probably decided that they were not worth the possible sacrifice, and if that were the case, then the only honorable thing would be to oppose the entire endeavor, not to support it with the blood of other people's sons.

These speculations are important for an understanding of what happened to me, of the choices I made. As the war did in fact drag on and on, year after year, with very few signs that either side was interested in ending its participation on terms that would be acceptable to the other, the likelihood that I would have to face my own Vietnam decision was increasing. In retrospect, the crisis that the war provoked in my family—which resulted in my mother having to relive her experience as a survivor of the Holocaust—was tantamount to a storm that first appears on the distant horizon as a single innocent cloud, but has an inevitability that becomes more and more apparent with each passing moment. The continuation of the war, despite the protests, the marches, the passionate debates that divided families, the Senate hearings, Gene McCarthy, the Tet Offensive, Bobby Kennedy, the Chicago convention, Vietnamization, and Kent State, propelled the storm inexorably from the horizon to a position directly overhead. When, at the beginning of my senior year in college, in December 1969, I drew number 68 in the first draft lottery, and it had already been announced that all those with numbers up to 190 should expect to be summoned, the storm was no longer someone else's problem. My worst fears—and perhaps those of my parents—had been realized. A war that had previously been confined to an area 10,000 miles away had come to my house.

It is difficult today to convey to those who did not live

through that sad and confusing time what it was like to be forced to devise a strategy to support one's decision not to fight in Vietnam. Depending on one's viewpoint, that choice was either honorable or cowardly, wise or traitorous, defensible or disgusting, smart or unpatriotic, to name a few labels that were then used. To those who were convinced that the purpose of the war was to preserve freedom, democracy, and the American Way of Life from Communist aggression, not wanting to go was asking someone else to jeopardize himself for your liberty. If, on the other hand, one thought that the war was about the arrogance of American power, and that the Vietnamese had a right to conduct their own affairs without interference from us, then not going was acting on one's convictions. Either way, the choice was not easy, and of course could be perilous.

Once I had decided that I could not and would not participate, I had to develop a plan that would make full use of the options available to me under the Selective Service System. The rules on deferments were constantly changing. When I started college, going to graduate school qualified as a deferment. By the time I was about to graduate, that deferment was gone. I had already rejected the options of joining campus ROTC or the army reserves, because by a certain point I wanted nothing whatsoever to do with the military—the war machine as it was called by many—though exercising either of those options almost certainly meant that one wouldn't be drafted and sent to Vietnam to fight. But I was too militantly anti-war to consider that route.

After drawing my unlucky lottery number, I had to act

quickly. I was already engaged to be married the following May, and I spoke with Judy's father, who was—ironically—a retired army colonel, to see if there was anything he could do to get me out of the draft. As a supporter of the war, he found it difficult to empathize with my strident moral scruples, but he did offer to try to get me into a good reserve unit. That was the last time we ever discussed the war or my desire not to fight in it.

I then met with a professor on campus who was known as a vocal anti-war activist and who also acted as a draft counselor. I quickly realized that his moral scruples did not include "working the draft system," and that the only principled thing to do as far as he was concerned was to be drafted and resist. Somehow, going to jail to make a point was not part of my game plan either, although I had deep admiration for those who had the courage to choose that path. I was not, however, among them.

At the start of my senior year, anticipating that I was about to face serious draft problems even before I drew the potentially deadly number 68, I had enrolled in a course that would enable me to get an interim certificate to teach in the Philadelphia public schools, not something I necessarily wanted to do, but something I would do to avoid getting drafted. Teachers were deferred. This seemed to me to be a relatively painless route to my goal, given the fact that I was graduating in the spring, was getting married, and had no career plans other than making sure I stayed out of the armed forces. But then, in April 1970, a month before I was to graduate, the Selective Service System announced that it would no longer be granting deferments to teach. I had run out of easy options. From a single benign cloud far off on the horizon, the storm was now a full force hurricane, and I was the eye.

I discussed the situation with my parents and they fully supported my decision to retain the services of a prestigious Philadelphia law firm, one of whose members specialized at that time in draft law. Over the summer, after I graduated and got married, as expected I was reclassified 1A, eligible to be drafted. But at least now I had help.

My attorneys were astute, knowledgeable, and encouraging. They systematically reviewed my case, and found three potential areas, any one of which could result in the deferment I was now beginning to covet. The first was medical. As my physical examination to determine whether I was fit for service was rapidly approaching, this was the first point at which my march into the army could be stopped. The lengths to which young men went during the Vietnam era to avoid military service for medical reasons are by now legend—heavy drug use, letters from psychiatrists indicating mental illness, feigned homosexuality, starving oneself to be underweight, stuffing oneself to be overweight, and so on. In my case, I have a congenital defect in my left thumb. It cannot go flat. Although it has unrestricted mobility toward my palm, it cannot move away from it. My attorneys joked that it would have been better had I been left-handed, but at bottom, these cases are arbitrary, with examining doctors having a great deal of individual leeway to decide deferments. My attorney suggested I visit an orthopedic surgeon, who would examine my thumb and write up a report. I was now well into my first firefight of my own Vietnam—the war I would fight with the Selective Service System.

If I passed the physical, which at this point was still a question mark, there was then the matter of my convictions. I knew I was passionately against the war, and had participated in various protest activities over the years, so I passed my bona fides in that respect. But the law was clear. In order to be granted conscientious objector status, and perform community, rather than military, service, one had to prove that one opposed all wars, not just a particular one. Could that be done? My attorneys thought so, even though I had not demonstrated against a war other than the one in Vietnam. But these considerations could wait, since our strategy was to work on one potential deferment at a time.

The third possibility, and, according to my attorneys, the most compelling, was to seek a deferment based on my mother's experiences during World War II. The knowledge of her plight was one of my earliest memories. At the age of twelve, the youngest of four children in a Jewish family in Vienna, she was sent via the Red Cross–arranged *Kindertransport* to England shortly after the *Anschluss,* the German annexation of Austria in 1938. Her entire family—mother, brothers, sister, aunt, uncle, and cousins—perished in Nazi death camps. The only other family member to survive was her father, Pop Pop Peter, as I called him, who by a twist of fate was out of Austria on business when the borders of Europe were closed, and who tried in vain to secure safe passage out of Vienna for the rest of his family. Although my mother and Pop Pop Peter remained in London for the duration of the war, they could not live as father and daughter, since my grandfather's flight forced him to adopt a false name under an assumed identity. My mother lived with a Jewish family in London, withstanding the Blitz, met my father, an American GI, and came to the United States after their wedding in 1945.

The story of her tragic circumstances is significant, for the Selective Service System at that time could grant a deferment if, in its opinion, there was some sort of dependency of a family member on a draft-age son. In most cases this deferment was granted for financial reasons, which was not the case here, or if the young man in question was the sole surviving son of a family that had lost other men in combat, which also didn't apply. But draft boards were known to grant dependency deferments to the sons of Holocaust survivors. It was by no means automatic, and each board made its own decision in each case, but my attorneys were quite convinced that if the other two possibilities failed, then this one would surely work.

When it came time for my physical examination, which took place at the end of the summer, I gave the orthopedic surgeon's report regarding my thumb to the examining physician. He read it, wiggled my thumb, and asked me if it hurt. When I replied that it didn't, he made a notation in my file, and went on to ask a few more questions. At the end of the exam, he said I would hear from them, and indeed I did. A few weeks later I received a notice that I had passed the physical. I was still 1A, eligible to be inducted into the armed forces of the United States.

With one of three possible deferments used up, we focused on the next one with a bit more urgency. As I began my new job as a sixth-grade teacher in an inner-city school in Philadelphia, the real focus of my life was the draft drama that was slowly unfolding. I immediately applied for conscientious objector status, filled out and submitted the requisite forms, and received a date at which I was to appear before the draft board to answer questions about my petition.

On the day before my scheduled appearance, I met with my attorneys to review the parameters of the law. I was to say that I could not imagine any war in which I could involve myself as a combatant. If I were asked what wars I had protested, I was to answer Vietnam because that's the only war I'd known. If they asked whether I would have protested American involvement in World War II or the Korean War, I was to say that the question was purely hypothetical and that I could not say for sure.

I then asked one of my attorney's something that was troubling me. What if they asked what I would do if someone broke into our apartment in the middle of the night and started to attack me and my wife? I don't know what it was that bothered me about that question, but I knew I needed some clarification. My attorney replied that defending oneself and one's wife had nothing whatsoever to do with war and that I was to reply that I would do whatever it took to defend myself. His answer satisfied me and I felt confident that I could achieve my goal—that I would be granted the deferment. It was even likely that my position as a teacher in an impoverished neighborhood would qualify as community service, which in fact it was.

The interview went well. The five board members were

cordial, straightforward, and businesslike. Each of them in turn asked questions about my convictions, my moral beliefs, my pacifism, and how I came to hold these views. Sure enough, they asked if I had ever protested any other wars, and sure enough, they asked what I would do if I were to be confronted with an intruding attacker who was intending to hurt me and rape my wife. I responded quickly that while I was against all wars, the latter scenario was not combat and that, like any person, I would do whatever I could to defend myself and my wife. They thanked and dismissed me, and as I was confidently walking out of the room, I heard, for the second time in my two dealings with the Selective Service System, that I would "hear from" them.

For whatever reason, I didn't hear from them. Weeks passed and there was not a single word—one way or the other—from the draft board. My life was beginning to take on an anxious, pins-and-needles quality, and every day as I came home from my job, my heart would beat wildly as I reached into the box for the mail. But still there was no news. I could do nothing to relieve the tension, as it was common knowledge that under no circumstances was one to contact the draft board for any reason, since there was always the possibility, as the Selective Service System had a much-deserved reputation for inefficiency, that one's file had been lost or misplaced. Thus it was considered stupid to remind them of one's existence. No news was good news, and as each day passed without word, I began to relax. There is a deep and abiding part of me that is convinced that things will turn out the way I want them to, and that part took over and led me to feel a sense of safety for the first time in a year, since I had drawn that unfortunate 68 in the lottery.

Two months had passed since my appearance before the draft board, and Judy and I had settled into comfortable marital life when, three days before Christmas, 1970, I received a thick number 10 envelope from the Selective Service System. My ears pulsated with increased, adrenaline-induced circulation as I read the first two lines of the letter: "Greetings from the President of the United States. You are ordered to report for induction into the Armed Forces of the United States on January 10, 1971 . . ." I could read no further.

"What happened?" I exploded, the strain of the past year breaking my usually calm demeanor. "This must be a mistake. They can't draft me. They never said anything about being a conscientious objector. How could they do this? Those bastards! Those fucking bastards!"

Something had indeed gone wrong. While it was obvious that I had been denied CO status, I had never been informed of the draft board's decision. The law stipulated that all decisions on conscientious objector status were subject to appeal to the state draft board, which could overturn the ruling of the local board. I had never appealed because I had never been informed, and so the induction order came as a complete surprise. And now I had nineteen days to do something before I was scheduled to report.

My attorney requested and obtained an injunction against the induction, and a court date was set for late January. I asked for and received a copy of the file concerning my CO petition. There was a three-page transcript of my interview, which included a one-paragraph decision at the bottom of the third page. It stated that although I had claimed to be opposed to all wars, I had protested only the war in Vietnam, and that even though I claimed to be against violence, I would defend myself if I were attacked. Their recommendation was that I be denied my application to be a conscientious objector.

Well, that paragraph took care of one piece of the puzzle—their decision—but it left the other piece—*informing me* of their decision—missing. It was at this point that I was first introduced to the arcane nature of the law. Since we were the plaintiffs, bringing an action against the government for drafting me illegally (that is, that they had not told me of their decision, giving me the right to appeal), we had the burden of proof. The government did not have to prove that they sent notification of their decision, we had to prove that they didn't. Since correspondence from the draft board went out in ordinary first-class mail, there was no record of the offending letter being either sent or received. But at least my induction order was postponed, and even if the judge's eventual ruling was unfavorable, there was still the opportunity to prepare the third—and final—argument for a deferment, based on my mother's experience during World War II.

My court appearance before a judge whose brother was a Spanish teacher at my high school was an exercise in futility. Under orders from my attorney, I cut my dark, thick, beautiful Afro, shaved off my mustache and beard, and parted my hair on the side as I had worn it up until four years before. In retrospect, this was completely irrelevant, since the judge never once looked at me during the entire one-hour proceeding. He betrayed no humor, no sentimentality, no emotion. He was all business. I testified under oath that I had not received the notice, and the secretary of the draft board testified under oath that she had sent it. The judge ruled that the burden of proof was on us and that we hadn't proved our assertion. He said that the induction order was legitimate and that I was to remain 1A.

I was now slipping down to my last card. As I received my application for the dependency deferment, Judy and I began to discuss the very real possibility that we would be forced by an unfavorable outcome to emigrate to Canada, which was at that time relatively easy to do, if one had skills and education. We discussed this with my parents, who were supportive of the idea, knowing that there was the likelihood that I could never return to the United States. This would certainly be another irony. It was the United States to which my mother came because of war, and it would be the United States I would leave for the same reason. We never discussed this possibility with Judy's parents, since they had no idea I was in any kind of jeopardy regarding the draft, and certainly would not have looked favorably on their daughter being spirited away by her "fuzzy-haired, hippie, left-wing" husband to an uncertain future in a foreign country, which would have been their view.

But there was still the matter of the deferment, and we began the laborious process of convincing the draft board, which I now considered to be my personal enemy, that my mother's experience as a Holocaust survivor was sufficiently horrible to warrant not having to face the possible loss of another close family member.

It was then that my mother had to return to hell—a world she had spent her entire life trying to leave. Since the draft board required all manner of documentation, proof in effect that her experiences really happened, she was forced to dredge up materials and mementos about her family that I never knew existed. Letters, photos, and official papers were inspected with meticulous care to determine if they could be useful in saving me from an uncertain future. And of course this immersion in a world that was her reality just thirty years before set off an intense emotional outburst that I had never previously seen. She cried constantly. Each photo, each letter, each document, each memento seemed to bring forth a memory, a regret, an anecdote, an insight that would inevitably be accompanied by tears. And of course the rest of us could not help but be shaken by the sight of my mother breaking down whenever another item was examined.

Then finally she came across what she was looking for. Among her many papers were documents issued by the Vienna city hall stating that her mother and siblings were sent to a camp somewhere in Eastern Europe and, the document went on euphemistically to state, "never heard from again."

My feelings about the Selective Service System, and the government it represented, suddenly went ballistic. I hated them. From Nixon on down, I detested what they were doing in Vietnam, and what they were doing to the fragile emotional state of my mother, me, and the rest of the family. Why couldn't they just leave me alone? Here I was, twenty-two years old, married, willing to endure teaching school in one of the worst crime-ridden areas of Philadelphia. Conditions at this place were so bad that periodically the principal would inform us over the loudspeaker to keep the kids in the classrooms when the final bell rang because two gangs were confronting each other in the school yard with chains and clubs. And amidst these conditions I was there day after day, trying to teach these kids how to read, write, and use numbers, how to behave themselves, how to treat other people, how to respect themselves and the world around them, showing them what it was like to be turned on by learning. Yes, here I was, the son of a woman who had managed to survive unspeakable horrors at the age of twelve, and this arrogant, insensitive, yes, murderous government, *my government,* would not leave me alone, would not let me live and work and love in peace, kept at me like some relentless hound that would not let go of the scent. Why was I so important to the war effort? What was it about me that aroused them so? This experience was beginning to change me forever. If this was the way I was being dealt with, the son of a privileged middle-class suburban family, a family that was immune from hardship and deprivation, that had the resources to hire attorneys and the savvy to work the system, I for the first time could imagine what it must be like to be underprivileged in this country, to be without the financial or intellectual resources to deal adequately with this overweening machine.

But I still had work to do, and I submitted the required documents: proof that my mother's family died in the camps, a letter from her doctor detailing my mother's ailments, which included hypertension, a note from our rabbi about the impact that World War II had on the survivors, and a statement from me asking in no uncertain terms that the draft board take into account the gravity of this psychological and emotional situation and look favorably on my request.

I was called again to appear. The interview was tense. We were now locked in a kind of combat of our own. Who would blink first? I had no idea what they thought of me personally, but the fact that I was back before them meant that, if they could, they were going to try to draft me. My only chance was that they would have pity for my mother, and try not to add to her unpleasant memories of war and the burden she would carry for the rest of her life by insisting that I be drafted. Despite the increasing tension, we were confident that this ordeal would be over soon, especially after the draft board called my mother in and asked her to recount her experiences as a twelve-year-old girl in Vienna. She told them. She talked about neighbors, whom she had known all her life and who were friendly and cordial, suddenly spitting at her and calling her dirty Jew after the Nazis took over in 1938, and how proud, educated, sophisticated men and woman were humiliated by young bullies with the imprimatur of the government, and forced to get down on their hands and knees and scrub sidewalks with toothbrushes.

She also had to tell them about her family, how even after she was relatively safe in London, sitting night after night on an assigned seat in the Underground dodging the German bombardment, she had corresponded with family members until 1942, when the letters stopped, and that it was only after the war was over in 1945 that she found out that they had perished.

When the interviews were over, for the third time I heard the familiar refrain—I would hear from them. I managed a smile and couldn't help but wonder if they would send any future correspondence to me by registered mail, return receipt requested.

As before, days turned into weeks. We heard nothing. Some days were easier to bear than others, but again as before, it was still considered ill-advised to contact the draft board and inquire about my case. The anxiety level in my family reached record proportions. An unfavorable decision meant total disruption, an abrupt flight to Canada to begin another existence as a "landed immigrant." A favorable decision meant that I could close this chapter of my life, that in some way the ignominious deaths of my mother's family could be redeemed if their passing could enable me to live in my own country with my convictions intact. But no news at all was becoming a grinding burden.

This tense and unstable atmosphere was lightened only by the presence of my grandfather, who had remarried after the war and moved to Atlantic City, not far from us. Pop Pop Peter was an engaging, debonair man, with an Old World charm. We were extremely close, and each time I saw him I could feel his humor, his warmth, his tenderness. He was a link to the past, to the life that my mother and her family had lived before the nightmare began. It was impossible to know from his affable demeanor of the horrific experiences he had endured during the war, and it was clear that he adored my brother and me. To him, we were special, the only grandchildren of his only surviving child, and he indulged us and hugged us and kissed us as if he could undo that past with his affection. We often stayed with him at the shore, where he was a chef, and at times he would come up to Philadelphia to visit with us, which was the case while we were waiting for the notification from the draft board.

Although he was seventy-five and had suffered a heart attack some years before, he had recovered and was able to resume a normal life. But it was impossible to be around my family and not be taken in by the tension of my situation. My mother of course had explained to him what was going on, and one day, while he and I were alone, he said he wanted to talk to me. In a totally deliberate manner, he pulled out a worn and faded picture of a young man in uniform, leaning against a rather large artillery shell. I asked him who that was and he said it was "your grandfather." He proceeded to recount some of his experiences in the army of Emperor Franz Joseph of Austria-Hungary during World War I, and said that since he knew how to be a soldier, I should tell the army to take him instead of me. "I'll go for you," he kept saying over and over, until we both started to laugh, the humor of his idea finally getting to him as well. It was probably the lightest moment I had experienced in six months.

And then one day the wait was over. As soon as I saw two letters from the Selective Service in the mailbox—one being a very thick one—I knew that my days as a resident of the United States were numbered. It was a Friday in May 1971, and I was already mentally putting into place the Canada plan when I opened the thinner of the two envelopes. The letter was short: "We have denied your petition for deferment based on dependency. It is the unanimous decision of the draft board that you be inducted into the Armed Forces of the United States." At this point the only reason to open the second letter was to find out how much time I had before having to flee. For the second time in six months I had been drafted, but in contrast to the first time, I was now out of options. The game was over.

I called my mother, who was so distraught she could not speak. I went to my parents' house and in grave tones told them that the only alternatives left to me were Canada and prison and that I was committed to the former. I would of course call the lawyers on Monday, but there was really nothing much at this point that anyone could do. My attorneys were in favor of resistance, but by now I wanted to get on with my life, even if it was in another country. In truth, it was fine with me because at that point I no longer had any more love for my own.

Like Alice, I had passed through the looking glass. My worst fears had materialized. All the planning, the preparation, the strategy sessions, the hoping had turned out to be of no avail in the face of the persistence of the government of the United States of America. It could do what it wanted to in Vietnam, and with me. They had won. I had lost.

The next day was strangely serene. Judy and I talked heart to heart, and I told her that if she wanted to stay behind, I would understand. She was now going to have to tell her parents about our secret life, and she pledged her unequivocal support. She maintained that going to Canada was not the worst thing that could happen to her. We got out the map and traced the route to Toronto with a yellow marker. She was on board.

That night we visited with Jack and Jane, our closest friends, to tell them of the news. We realized that these moments together, which we had always taken for granted, were now infinitely more precious. The mood was oddly turning into one of merriment, even of excitement, at the thought of our impending new life, when the phone rang and Jack answered it.

"It's for you," he said, handing me the receiver. "It's your father."

I took the phone. "What's up, Dad."

"Pop Pop Peter had a stroke," he said in a solemn tone. "Your mother told him that you and Judy were going to have to leave the United States and live in Canada, and a few hours later he collapsed."

I truly could not believe what I was hearing. "Oh my God, how is he?"

"Not good. He's in a coma at Holy Redeemer Hospital and the doctors don't think he's going to make it."

"This is too much. How is Mom?"

"She's taking it pretty hard."

T. S. Eliot makes reference somewhere to events being in the saddle. I know exactly what he means. There are moments in any life when all the intention one brings to bear on a situation seems puny in comparison to the might of circumstances. All thought of the draft, my impending induction date, and crossing the border into Canada were banished from my consciousness, replaced only by anguish over my grandfather's deteriorating condition. We waited in vain for him to regain consciousness. He never did, passing over to the other side a few days after the stroke. The last words he had said to me were "I'll go for you."

While my family made arrangements for the funeral, I was once again in contact with my attorneys. Under their instructions, I informed the draft board of my grandfather's death, asking it to postpone my induction and, given this most recent development, reopen my dependency case. The draft board in turn asked that I submit a death certificate, which I did, and then sent me a postponement. The letter did not mention anything about my status, but by this time we had learned to take things one step at a time. While we all began to grieve the loss of Pop Pop Peter, the mourning was framed by the temporary gaining of my freedom. For the moment, I had no obligation to the Selective Service System, although I fully expected to be sent another notice in the following month's call-up. My plan was to use my grandfather's passing as a way of finally putting this nightmare behind me.

This period of my life was the most emotionally complex I had ever experienced. I had heretofore not understood what the real meaning of the word "bittersweet" was. In the space of a few weeks I had been drafted, had made plans to leave the country—probably forever, had endured the death of my grandfather, was granted a second reprieve from the draft, and was waiting apprehensively for the moment when I would have to face the dogs again.

As the end of June approached, I allowed myself to exhale, since I had not been called to report for induction for a

third time. I have no idea why I was passed by. I could specu-
late that the draft board had lost its will to contend with me
after Pop Pop Peter's death, but it is impossible to know for
sure. And of course I never called them to find out why they
hadn't drafted me. Earlier in the spring I had been accepted as
a graduate student in history for the fall semester at New
York University, and Judy and I tentatively began to make the
necessary arrangements to move to New York. Although we
had no idea what was ultimately going to happen to us, at least
we knew that for the moment we were going to be starting a
new life—and it wasn't going to be in Toronto.

It was then that the United States government, another
part of which had been so fervent in its desire to have me participate in its bloody enterprise, inadvertently stepped in to
help my cause. By this time the Senate was full of anti-war
sentiment, and a group of senators succeeded in filibustering a
bill that contained an extension of the Selective Service System. On June 30, 1971, the draft expired, and it was unclear
when it would resume. In the meantime, no one would be
drafted, and since American involvement in the ground war
was rapidly diminishing, the feeling in political circles was
that there wasn't a need to fill many more slots. At least for
now I was no longer in any immediate danger, and in late
August we moved to Greenwich Village, where I began to live
a life that I had freely chosen.

Although I had informed the draft board of my move,
which was required by law, there was something about living in a new apartment in a new city with a whole new set of
circumstances that made me feel immune, even when the

draft was reinstated in the fall. There was no particular reason to feel this way—my classification was still 1A—but somehow the events of the previous spring seemed far, far removed from my everyday concerns. I was now busy studying the trenchant works of Giordano Bruno, Sir Francis Bacon, and Thomas More, and the interconnected causes of the English Revolution of the seventeenth century. Somehow all the draft woes seemed to be part of a chapter of my life that I had already closed—Pop Pop Peter was gone, buried, and mourned, the war was winding down, and I was still a resident of the United States, studying to get my doctorate in history.

The storm, which had been the principal reality of my life since I drew that ill-fated 68, had passed and was now moving to another horizon. Perhaps the draft board had finally grown tired of me. We were like two heavyweight boxers slugging it out, and after I received the second induction order I had conceded defeat to them. But I was yet to realize that life almost always provides additional rounds in which to contend. We were both bloodied by the bout, had fought to a draw, and now it was time to turn to healing our wounds. Or perhaps this wasn't the case at all, perhaps it was merely a matter of God looking at me and my emotionally wrung-out family and, as with Job, saying, "Enough."

The year turned and now the draft problems I had experienced seemed to be part of another lifetime. Judy and I settled contentedly into our new lives as the country's involvement in the war was confined to dropping thousands of tons of bombs on North Vietnam from B-52s a mile up in the heavens.

Since I was not a pilot and there was very little likelihood I was going to become one, I was relatively safe.

And then, lying in bed one morning in the spring of 1972 listening to the news on the radio, I heard a ten-second item that seemed to be from a script that I would have written had I been given the chance: "The Pentagon announced today that all those who were eligible to be drafted in 1971—and weren't—would be placed in a second-priority pool. Their chances of being drafted now are negligible." I could hardly believe what I had just heard. My spirits soared. They were talking about me. I was certainly eligible to be drafted in 1971. And then I came back down to earth. But maybe they weren't talking about me. I *was* drafted, even though I wasn't inducted. Maybe this doesn't apply. But even if it doesn't, if they wanted to draft me, wouldn't they have done so by now? I called my lawyers.

They felt confident that I was now free and clear. Even though it was still impossible to make inquiries to the draft board about me specifically, their intelligence said that the fact that I had been drafted made no difference. They were 99 percent certain that this announcement applied to me.

Two weeks later I received the last piece of correspondence ever sent to me from the Selective Service System. It said that I had been reclassified 1H and that I wouldn't be drafted unless there was a mobilization of the scale of World War II. These people sure had a way with words. In some odd fashion the letter was thoroughly anticlimactic, almost an afterthought, like dotting an *i*. The game had been over for a long time now. Although there was continued death and destruction in Vietnam, including the infamous Christmas bombing of the North in 1972, for me the war, which had troubled my consciousness and that of my family since Lyndon Johnson first sent American troops into combat in the spring of 1965, had ended.

And when I reflect on these events, which I occasionally do, I can't help but visualize the den in my parents' house in which Pop Pop Peter showed me the photo of himself in the emperor's army, with a knowing look in his eyes, saying over and over, "I'll go for you, I'll go for you." Forgive my sentimentality, but I can't help thinking that he did.

If my story were a Greek tragedy, Pop Pop Peter would be my sacrifice, what I would have had to serve up to the gods as a way of sparing my own life. My situation was hopeless. I was headed for another country. The irony of the situation was not lost on me. I would have to leave the United States because I didn't agree with its policies, and it didn't agree with my opposition. It was a huge moral issue, one that a young man such as I had no previous experience facing.

But then I was handed the marvelous gift of freedom by my beloved grandfather, who chose the most opportune moment to leave this life that anyone could have imagined. It was as if he had willed himself to the other side just to spare my mother and me any further agony—that in his view his family had suffered enough and it was now time to relieve the pain.

I miss him a lot, and can't thank him enough for what he did. And I hope I have the opportunity at some point to tell him this personally.

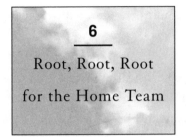

6

Root, Root, Root
for the Home Team

ALTHOUGH WATCHING AND follow-
ing professional sports had been a major part of my life, I had
no way of knowing that a new interest—ice hockey—would
show me the violent, ugly side of competition, and lead me
away from a passion that had been so much a part of my life
since I was a small boy.

Ice hockey had never figured into my personal equation,
mostly because Philadelphia did not have a National Hockey
League team. I knew about stars such as Gordie Howe and
Bobby Hull from reading sports magazines, but the game itself was foreign. Baseball, basketball, and football more than
occupied me. Hockey was a sport played in Canada by Cana-
dians, and since I didn't ice-skate, I had very little affinity for
the game.

All that changed in 1967 when the NHL expanded from
six teams to twelve, and Philadelphia was awarded one of the
franchises. It was at a time when my overall engrossment in

sports was peaking, and somehow the game caught the fancy of both my brother and me. Perry was completely smitten. He began to skate at the local rinks in the city, and follow the new team, the Flyers, identifying the players' names and faces and learning the rules. We also began to watch games on television, and on Christmas Eve of that year, when the Flyers beat the Kings on television, 2–0, to inaugurate the Forum in Inglewood, our house was a hockey house, and we were soon attending games and following the team on the radio.

Although I never became much of a skater, Perry got real good, real fast, and within a few years he was a goalie for one of the teams that had sprung up near our home in suburban Philadelphia. Although his team wasn't very good, he was. He had attended hockey camp deep in the woods of Ontario during the summers, and many professional players were there to teach the kids the finer points of the game. And since Perry always got good at something in which he was interested, before long he had real pads, a real glove, and real goalie skates. He was a hockey player. Our days of playing in the living room with a tennis ball were a thing of the past. He was competing with other fourteen- and fifteen-year-olds in a way that I could only admire, and admire I did.

On one cold night in the fall of 1970, I watched him play against a team that was obviously much better than his. There were perhaps a hundred fans in attendance and the game turned out to be one of those moments in sports that is completely unexpected, when what one is seeing transcends the ordinary. In all my years of watching hockey, and this now adds up to almost thirty, I have never seen a better performance by a goaltender before or since, and neither I'm sure would anyone else had they been there that night.

His team was completely overmatched, and the only thing that prevented the score from being twenty to nothing was my brother. He stopped shot after shot while his team could not get the puck out of its own end. His team's defense was nonexistent. Perry was the defense. The other team would pass the puck around to try to get an open shot but he would be there. They regularly took two and three and sometimes four shots in succession but Perry stopped every one of them. By the end of the second period the other team led 1–0 but my brother had stopped about 30 shots at that point, while his team had managed just two, one in each period. It didn't seem that there was any way his team could score, and in fact they didn't, getting two additional shots in the final period, while Perry let another goal in to make the final score 2–0.

The other team in the end had 45 shots. It was the slaughter of the innocents but I had seen something that in all the years of playing and watching sports I had never seen, and that was a young man not giving up in the face of overwhelming odds, never succumbing to the hopelessness of the situation. In the back of his mind, Perry knew that he could not win. His team could play all night and not get close to scoring. But he also knew that his job was to turn back the opposition and he accomplished that objective spectacularly, earning a spot in my heart for the rest of my life for his fortitude and perseverance, and earning a place in the heart of the opposing team's coach, who rushed out on to the ice to congratulate my brother as soon as the game was over, again something I had never seen before and have not seen since.

Sports always has the potential to elevate. That's what drew me to it early, and has stayed with me ever since. There is always the possibility while playing or watching that I or someone else would transcend our ability and do something that would on the surface seem to be impossible. An ordinary play always has the potential to become something extraordinary. Of course there was the competitive aspect as well, the idea that one team had to win and it could be the team I rooted for, although coming from Philadelphia at that time there was little likelihood of that. The city had a reputation for being a town of losers, and although there had been the odd championship—most recently in 1967 when the basketball 76ers conquered the loathed Boston Celtics after the Celtics had won ten or twelve titles—when people thought of Philly they thought of the baseball team, the Phillies, which had in its long and lackluster life never won a world series, never, not once. That seemed to characterize Philadelphia, and when the Flyers settled into comfortable mediocrity, no one seemed to notice. In fact it was expected of a Philadelphia team.

But by the end of 1973 that had changed. The Flyers had been improving steadily, and the return of goaltender Bernie Parent, who had been with the team at the beginning but had been traded away, was the last link in the development of what was to become a championship team. But no one knew that at the time, and although the Flyers were winning, very few fans took them seriously—except us.

We were big fans by that point, and while I lived in New York and the Flyers were in Philly, we still rooted for them, strongly. And in fact, since my wife, Judy, worked for the National Hockey League offices directly above Madison Square Garden, hockey was a big part of our life. We attended lots of games, sitting in the same seats year after year, and rooted openly for the Flyers. But the New York team, the Rangers, was bigger, faster, and better than the Flyers for most of that period, and was able to prevail over our guys almost every time we watched them play at the Garden.

At least that was the case the first two years during which we went to the games. By the third year, the 1973–74 year, the Flyers now had Bernie Parent, and the first game of the season between the two teams in November was turning out to be a tight, taut affair, with both teams playing very hard. We rooted just as long and just as loud as we normally did, but for the first time I noticed that some local fans in the row in front of us were not taking too kindly to our cheers.

With the score tied late in the game, and with a lot of physical play between the two teams, I sensed hostility emanating from in front, and no amount of joking and jibing seemed to ameliorate it. When the Flyers scored very late in the game to win 3–2, Judy and I erupted in joy, but we were met with icy stares from down below. Season after season the Rangers had come close to winning a championship but hadn't succeeded since 1940, more than thirty years before, and so Rangers fans had their own sense of frustration that the up-start Flyers were now adding to. As we filed out of the cavernous, silent arena, I was happy that my team had won but feeling the pressure to contain my satisfaction, sensing that I was in enemy territory. All of Judy's co-workers were of course Rangers fans, and we had taken a lot of good-natured ribbing over the years about how bad our team was. On this night we could give it back to them a little, but we waited until the fans from the row in front were safely out of earshot before indulging. Something told me to be discreet, that it wasn't safe to be open about my support for the visiting team. It was the first time in my life that I realized how personally some people take sports, that it matters so much to them that they can become hostile over the outcome of a contest.

Judy and I attended many more games during that season at the Garden without incident, but I was there merely as a spectator, since deep down I couldn't have cared less who won between the Rangers and the Canadiens or the Rangers and the Penguins. I sat and watched and cheered good plays, but my heart was with the Flyers, who played ninety miles away and who were doing very well, winning game after game with tough defense, outstanding goaltending, and physical intimidation. They became known as the Broad Street Bullies, and as the regular season was coming to an end, they seemed to have as good a chance as any team to do well in the play-off rounds that led to the Stanley Cup championship. As my marriage of nearly four years was slowly deteriorating, it seemed that the last thing that held us together, the only thing Judy and I had in common, was our love for the Flyers and the pleasure we took in seeing the team succeed. Hockey was Judy's life, but although I enjoyed it, it was by no means the most important thing in mine. But it was a great diversion, and when the Flyers blew right by the first team they played in the play-offs without losing a game, as luck would have it the next team on their schedule was the Rangers. For the time being, our marriage was being held together by ice hockey.

The first two games were played in Philadelphia and the Flyers won them handily. The series was now returning to New York for the next two games, and of course Judy and I were completely psyched about being able to see our team play the hometown Rangers in the Garden. The atmosphere around the building was tense, and all day Judy had to defend the Flyers as the Rangers fans with whom she worked verbally ganged up on her. But the Philly team did have a two games to none lead in the series, and all it needed to do was win two more games and it would advance to the final, championship round.

We arrived at the Garden for the first game and sat in our regular seats. I had already decided that it wasn't a good idea to root openly or draw any attention to myself. Regular season games were one thing, but this was the play-offs, and when the row in front filled up with the same guys who had taken Judy and me to task for rooting against the Rangers in a game five months before, I suspected that the evening might turn out to be a difficult one, especially since these guys were carrying huge sixteen-ounce beers and seemed to have been drinking before they arrived. After taking their seats, they turned around, looked at us, and said only two words, which were at that point the most contemptible words they could think of—"Flyers fans."

We were trapped. They knew and we knew this was true. They had seen and heard us before, rooting for a team to defeat their beloved Rangers. And now that the Rangers were already two games down, they would be eliminated if they lost just two more. That night's game was critical.

I could see that their testy mood was real, that they were pissed off at how things had developed so far, and that they weren't happy to be sitting in front of a couple of Flyers fans. I tried to placate them with the old bromide about the best team winning, but they were in no mood to be humored. They said something back about us being prepared to fight for our team, but I didn't know what they were talking about. They were continuing to make veiled references about threatening us physically when Pat Casey, who was the husband of one of Judy's co-workers and a tough Hell's Kitchen New York Irishman and a die-hard Rangers fan himself, started to jaw back. He told the guys to turn around, shut up, and leave us alone, and their response was to immediately put him— mistakenly—in the same category with us—the enemy. As the game began to heat up on the ice, the tension around us seemed ready to explode. Although I had waited for this moment for so long, finally seeing a team I had followed for years actually have a chance to go all the way, I began to fear for my safety. Perhaps I should hope for a Rangers victory. Perhaps it was better to make sure that the thugs in front were happy than it was for me to be happy—and hurt. They were now on their third beer and when the Flyers scored the first goal of the game, they again turned around, pointed at and insulted us, and for the second time in a few minutes informed us point-blank that we needed to be prepared to fight for our team.

Every ounce of enjoyment had long since departed from

me. The tension in the building was so overwhelming—the collective hostility of thousands of angry people, mostly men—that objects were flying onto the ice. Fans were screaming madly at the Flyers, who were screaming back. It seemed that at any moment pandemonium was going to break out in the stands, and to top off this general sense of things being out of control, three toughs were menacing us personally. I was hardly paying any attention at this point to the game, but I did manage to glance at the ice just in time to see the Flyers put another shot into the Rangers net. The score was now 2–0 and in an instant, twenty years of being a sports fan, of enjoying the action, the competition, the buildup to the outcome, exploded in my face.

The three guys had turned around and lunged for Judy and me. Beer splashed everywhere. They tried to climb over the seats to grab us, but within moments bodies were in motion and they couldn't seem to get close. I had never been assaulted before, and my own reaction to what was happening was both puzzling and transforming. I just sat there. I didn't move an inch as ushers, policemen, other fans, and my defender Pat Casey battled directly above me. It was as if I had decided to absent myself completely from the altercation, as if I could ensure my physical safety by blanking out everything happening around me. I couldn't make out what was being said but people were shouting from all sides. Judy had run into the aisle, her hands over her mouth in horror and amazement that the three guys, drunk, angry, and frustrated, had chosen to take it all out on us. And I could also see Pat, his back pressed against his seat, his legs outstretched, trying to keep our assailants at bay with his feet.

I was twenty-five years old, and had played sports and been a sports fan all my life, and I can say in all honesty that never before had I considered the ugly side of sports, the side that draws to it en masse frustrated males who see sports as an outlet for their anger or their bitterness or God knows what else. In that moment all the love of sports I had cultivated since I was five years old disappeared. I wanted to have nothing in common with those three guys. I knew I could never take sports as seriously as I had in the past, that to care as much as I had cared before was a sickness that could lead to the disease I was witnessing in the hateful faces of my attackers. How empty, to have thought that somehow their lives could be redeemed if they were able to do in the stands what their team could not do on the ice.

And there I sat as the squall began to quiet down, as the ushers and the police removed these guys from their seats. I settled back to try to recapture the feeling of why I was there to begin with, and I couldn't understand what it was. And so I got up and left. The enjoyment I had derived from this particular culture was gone, and so I gathered up my wife and walked out into the lovely spring night.

I was happy to be away from it, happy that I had not been hurt or maimed, happy that people had come to my defense, and happy to have been relieved of an illusion—the myth that one can separate the violence inherent in competition from the violence that resides inside of us. I knew then that they were connected, and that my own need to compete and win, which had been a fairly strong element of my life, was connected to an inner lack that could never be compensated for with victories on the field or in other arenas. To be truly victorious was to have a sense of inner peace that had nothing to do with victory and defeat, winners and losers. And although those three guys were not me, I could see enough of them in me to be horrified by the possibility that I could feel the same emptiness they felt—that I would not choose their actions but the feeling would be the same. When I walked out of Madison Square Garden that night more than twenty years ago, I left part of me behind, the part that had chosen to overlook a very violent element that lurks just below the surface of professional sports. Violence is repulsive, even when it comes with a cloak of respectability.

The Rangers did come back to win that game, and I've often wondered what would have happened had we remained in the Garden and the outcome had been different. I'll never know, because two days later, when the second game was being played, I was home listening to it on the radio. I had already made much progress in my evolution from a rabid sports fan: before, given the opportunity, I would have attended the game; now, with the possibility of danger, I did not. Who knows if the three bullies would have been there, and if so, what they would have done? And who could have predicted in advance what the score of the game would be, whether Rangers fans would have been in a good mood or a bad one? What is clear is that I had been intimidated, that fear of physical violence over a hockey game had forced me to the sidelines, and when the Rangers won Game 4 to even the series, the fan in me, who had been an intimate part of my fabric for years and years, began to consider the possibility that my team, which had started so well, would lose. Given what had already transpired, I wondered how I would feel about that.

The series was hard-fought, tough, and evenly matched, and the seventh and final game was to be played in Philadelphia. Judy secured a ticket for me and on a sunny spring Sunday afternoon I found myself once again in the stands enjoying the play on the ice—this time in friendly territory. When the Flyers pulled out a thrilling 4–3 victory, my own eruption of glee was due in no small part to the fact that I was actually able to stand up and cheer at all. It was a relief to be able to pull for the team I happened to root for without fear of attack, and somehow it was also poetic justice that the victory of the Flyers was due in no small part to the fact that they could intimidate the Rangers on the ice. It's very hard to score in hockey if you are afraid to touch the puck out of fear that a great big body check awaits you if you do. Hockey can be a violent game, and maybe the physical part of the game encourages its fans to display this behavior in the stands. I am not a sports psychologist, merely a fan, but I do know that play in all major sports has gotten rougher over the years. I don't know if that is a mirror of what has gone on in society at large or the other way around.

But suddenly, my interest in the play-offs, which in ordinary circumstances would have been at a fevered pitch, was not top priority. I was in the midst of studying for my comprehensives as a doctoral candidate, and hockey games, the Stanley Cup, the fights in the stands, and who won and who lost seemed distant. Yes, I followed the Flyers and they were now playing the final round, but somehow I was for the first time in my life detached from it. I had seen this happen before. One good friend in Philly, who was an old hockey fan and with whom I had gone to many games over the years, witnessed a spectacle that appalled him. The Flyers were playing the Canadiens, the fabled Montreal team whose hallmark was skilled passing and quick, clever skating, and were not only beating this team that had won the Stanley Cup something like twenty-four times, they were beating them up on the ice as well. My friend Gary, who was such a fan, who had followed the Flyers through years of futility, could not bring himself to enjoy what he considered a travesty of a game, even if the Flyers were benefiting from the the rough play. He walked out in the middle of the game and never returned to watch another one. His sensibilities were offended, and after the incident at the Garden, I understood.

In the final Stanley Cup round the Flyers had gone up three games to two and were a game away from becoming the champions of hockey—which would have made them the first expansion team to accomplish this feat. It would have been the equivalent of the Miracle Mets of 1969. The game was to be played in Philadelphia against the Boston Bruins, and, as would be expected, a ticket to the game was the hottest item in town. I had connections of course, and Judy was able to secure three tickets—for Perry, for my friend Ned, and for me—and we made our way down to the Spectrum to arrive in plenty of time at the WILL CALL window to pick up the treasured envelope.

Security was tight, and it was difficult just to get to the window, but I slowly made my way and sure enough there was an envelope with my name on it, and after showing two pieces of ID, I had the prized tickets in hand. When I looked inside, I saw only two tickets. Someone had goofed, either Judy or the ticket office, but that was irrelevant at this point. There was no way we could get another ticket, as the game had been sold out from the moment it was clear that it would be played, and there we were, three guys who had known one another for years and who all wanted to be inside to perhaps be a part of Philadelphia sports history.

There are moments when time does appear to stand still. For an instant we stood there looking into one another's faces to see if anyone was going to flinch and say that it wasn't all that important to go in, and no one did. That was the first thing that flashed through my mind. The second thing I remember was that a new tape began to play in place of the old one, which would have had me stand my ground and insist that it was my wife who had procured the tickets, and if one of us was not getting in to see the game, it wasn't going to be me. The second tape was entirely different. It said that all this excitement was shallow. This is what was going through my head as the three of us stood stock still, wondering who was going to blink first.

I did. I said that I didn't need to be there, that I would watch the game on television, and that I had no problem giving up my spot. Ned, with whom I had practically grown up, and who is as supportive a person as I've ever known, asked me ten times if I was sure I didn't want to go in, and each time I said I was sure I became more and more certain of that. It wasn't so much the sacrifice of a long-standing dream to be in the stands when the Flyers won the Stanley Cup, it was in part the recognition that these two guys meant a lot to me, so much so in fact that I could not see myself enjoying the game knowing that one of them would be on the outside. And I could also walk away because of the idea that the moment was in fact replaceable, that I had had a lot of moments in sports and could countenance the idea of watching the game on television as millions of others would do, because what mattered to me was not whether *I was there,* but whether the Flyers won. If they did, I would be happy, whether I was inside or out. If they lost, I would probably want to be on the outside.

I made my way to a friend's house after standing and watching Ned and Perry disappear into the crowd. Perry had a camera and promised to take pictures of the end of the game, if that was called for. The contest itself was once again close and nerve-wracking, and the Flyers were desperately trying to make the one goal they had scored in the first period hold up. Even though I found myself in a living room as we watched the game, I stood for most of the time. The idea of sitting down to watch was simply out of the question. When the final buzzer went off and the Flyers had won, 1–0, the entire city erupted. I caught up with Ned and Perry later and they told me what it was like to be in the arena. I found myself delighted that they had had such a good time, and to my surprise had no regrets about my decision not to go in.

I didn't go to the parade the next day, nor did I even consider it. And I never attended another hockey game in Madison Square Garden. The Flyers won another Stanley Cup the following year, but by then, divorced and in love with someone else, I paid only half attention to the games and in fact didn't even watch one on television, preferring instead a sensual evening of food, music, and lovemaking to the pretzels, beer, and cheering that characterized an evening in front of the tube.

We read stories about rabid sports fans running amok, soccer fanatics in Europe and elsewhere attacking the supporters of the opposing team. Every year people are killed at soccer matches because they happen to be associated with the wrong side. I actually witnessed this when I lived in London as a student in the seventies. On my street a few blocks away was a soccer stadium, and on the days when games were played, mounted police patroled the neighborhood, their assignment to keep rival fans away from one another. On game days, the neighborhood resembled a war zone.

Sports violence is merely an extension of violence in general. Some people cannot deal with their inability to influence their environment without resorting to physical threat. It is as if they haven't developed the necessary skills to persist without having to dominate. The world thus becomes a huge pecking order, with those in a position of strength menacing those with less, as they themselves are being treated roughly by someone above. This is why children bear the brunt of the inability of people to deal with their problems without resorting to violence.

The level of violence in sports has increased because the fans have demonstrated decisively that they want to see it. Every sport has gotten fiercer, more confrontational, more "in your face." But is this really so surprising? Isn't this the way we live now? The allure of violent resolutions, whether in sports or outside them, remains the same. It reflects the temptation to use physical power to exercise one's will, and in the case of athletes, who are bigger, faster, stronger, and more aggressive than ever, it is in competition that these skills can be utilized.

But violence always puts other ways of communicating—emotionally, verbally—in jeopardy. As people look more and more to violence to settle problems and differences, as the skills of compromise and cooperation are threatened, nonviolent solutions need even more support if they are not to go the way of the Edsel.

7

High School

Reunion

ONE OF THE by-products of a two-year relationship that began shortly after my divorce is that it got me out of New York. This might not seem to be a major accomplishment, but leaving New York is not always easy, even when one really wants to do it. There are things about it that are objectionable—crime, dirt, noise, crowds, attitude—but there are also things—arts, culture, hipness, excitement—that cannot be found to the same degree in any other American city. In many ways living in New York is like being involved in a dysfunctional relationship. As I used to say when I lived there—you can love it, but it will never love you.

So it turned out that a woman was the catalyst for me to say good-bye to New York and get on with the rest of my life. My romantic partner, Betsy, took a job in Washington, and for a year we carried on a long-distance relationship, which, as the Spanish proverb says, is a relationship of fools. We spent weekends together, ran up insupportably high phone bills, and tried our best to be a real couple—without much success. Our relationship had become pretty mystifying for both of us, but we continued on through inertia and a lack of appealing alternatives. We succumbed to the old trap of thinking that a bad relationship was better than no relationship at all.

In the meantime I had completed my doctorate in history and had landed a dinky job teaching Western Civilization in a small college in New Jersey to Vietnam veterans. Although satisfying in a way, it was not threatening to become a career position. I had applied for various jobs all over the country, perhaps twenty in all, and had not been granted an interview for any of them. So much the better, I thought, since by this point I was not at all enamored of the idea of being a university professor, even if I had no idea what else I wanted to or could do. I considered myself very much a New Yorker with progressive political views, and the idea of going to Stillwater, Oklahoma, or Huntsville, Texas, or Richmond, Indiana, without of course knowing anything about those places other than that they were west of the Hudson, demoralized me.

Then, in the spring of 1977, as my relationship with Betsy limped into its third year, and it seemed likely that I would continue to take the De Camp bus line from the Port Authority terminal in New York to my teaching gig in New Jersey, something happened that taught me two valuable lessons about living that I have never forgotten. One is that life is not an exercise that can be fully planned. Serendipity plays a large role. The second is that one never knows when certain skills or experiences that seem minor or insignificant can be pressed into service when one requires them the most.

I had by this time made friends with the partner of a woman who worked with Betsy, another floundering ex-academic, and he told me that with my skills (skills? what skills? I was a college teacher) I could get a job with the federal government as a writer, and that he knew who was hiring. I would make more money to start than I could being an itinerant scholar filling in for full professors on sabbatical for a year at a time in places I didn't want to live, I would be closer to Betsy, which we both agreed was a mixed blessing, and although Washington certainly wasn't New York, it wasn't Peoria either. I pursued his advice, and lo and behold I actually secured an interview with a female bureaucrat who seemed to be interested in me, who had a job opening, and who called me on a rainy, blustery Friday afternoon in March to offer me a position. I would start on May 3, earn a salary of $14,000, and be a writer.

I didn't have to think about it. I accepted on the spot, and she was delighted and said that the only hurdle was to "get you through civil service," whatever that meant. But she indicated that that was a formality, since she had already chosen me, and she told me to be there in six weeks.

All right! Way to go! Screw these Podunk colleges that couldn't spot a brilliant scholar and intellectual when they received his application. I was leaving the ivory tower and joining the "real world," with real money and a real job. I was taking advantage of the fact that I lived in the land of opportunity and was totally changing gears.

Betsy was ecstatic. Our intimate life improved immediately, and suddenly she was making noises about commitment and marriage, saying that she could never really imagine loving anyone else. I was getting my first lesson in how people are judged not by who they are, but by what they do—especially men. I thought I was the same person, but not to Betsy. Days before I was just another liberal arts Ph.D. with no prospects, political views that were far to the left of mainstream, and a member of a religion that did not accept Jesus Christ as Savior. Now I was on my way—oh, what irony, after what the government had put me through five years before—to becoming a Washington insider, a man with a respectable job and a bright future, and it was amazing to me that Betsy turned on her love light once again after it had been off for nearly a year and a half. Everything was right with the world, and I was even moving to a city in which I could get a cappuccino.

I gave notice at my job, let my landlord know I was leaving my apartment, and began to make arrangements to move. I got the letter of designation from Washington as had been promised, and was feeling very proud of myself. How clever of me to have turned a casual association and the ability to write grammatically acceptable sentences into a secure position. The plan was to move in with Betsy in Georgetown until I got situated, and then find my own place. I had led a carefully modest existence as a graduate student in New York, and now I was leaving the semi-bohemian world of Greenwich Village for a respectable middle-class life with Betsy in Washington, D.C. I even began to imagine our half-Jewish, half-Gentile kids running up and down the hall in a few years, but that certainly could wait.

About a week before I was to pick up the U-Haul and

drive myself and my limited possessions down the Jersey Turnpike to the nation's capital, I called my boss-to-be in D.C. It was not a great phone call. She said she still hadn't gotten clearance for me to work for her agency, and rather than report as scheduled, I should call when I arrived in town. She was rather blasé about the whole thing, telling me that the bureaucracy works very slowly just when you don't want it to, but after I hung up, I felt a twinge in the pit of my stomach. I was sure my teaching job was already filled, my apartment rented, and I was about to become a resident of Washington, whether I had a new job to go to or not.

Two days before moving, New York gave me a rousing send-off. On my way uptown to say good-bye to yet another friend, I heard a soft rumble on the Lexington Avenue subway train in which I was riding, which got louder as each moment passed. I looked up just in time to see a ventilation grate start to fall a few feet above my head. The metal grate began to swing down, and I braced myself for the expected shock and injury.

As luck would have it, the last of the four bolts held, and the grate stayed up, swinging back and forth as if it were a mad monkey, but I had the privilege of being showered with fifty years of accumulated dust, debris, and dirt. I was covered with soot, and I began to wipe myself furiously with my handkerchief as everyone around me both looked and did not look at the same time. This was a sign. When I had spent five minutes cleaning myself off, a Sikh, a man with a turban and a red dot in the middle of his forehead, slowly stood up, pointed to my cheek, and said in broken English, "Here, you missed a spot." I nodded at him and two days later I was no longer a New Yorker.

But was I really a Washingtonian? When I arrived in town and my contact in the government would not return my phone calls, I knew I was in deep trouble. And sure enough, a few days later a letter came to me with the return address of the agency that had "hired" me, indicating that the civil service had ranked me seventh in its listings of the people most suitable for "my" job, and I needed to be in the top five to be hired. Unless I was of all things a veteran, which I had expended a lot of energy in a successful attempt not to be, my job would have to go to someone else. I called my "boss," who said she had done all she could, wishing me a great rest of my life. I shook my head and said to myself that I should have known better than to expect anything good to come out of contact with those bastards.

Now what do I do? At least in New York I had a position in a field I knew something about, even if it wasn't about to be "permanent," whatever that meant. Betsy was as compassionate about this turn of events as Emperor Nero would have been. I was in a strange city with no contacts, no prospects, no idea of what I wanted to be when I grew up, and no money. I had spent the last twenty-three years of my life—since kindergarten—in a classroom, either as a student or a teacher, and I had no clue as to how to go about getting a job, much less working at one. It is difficult to convey to those who have not spent years in academia how isolated and removed it is from the rest of the world. I knew that I had to find out what the hell I wanted to do with my relationship with Betsy—to say nothing of my totally disjointed career ideas—and I could find that out only if we lived in the same city.

That we now did, but from the moment she learned of my failure to secure this position, she made it clear to me that I was not welcome in her place indefinitely, and that our very relationship was once again in question. The next two months were miserable. I furiously began to make calls to try to get something going that paid me a few bucks to live on, and I wondered to myself how I had managed to get into this position.

I investigated every possibility for a teaching position, but the few opportunities I could unearth wouldn't start until the fall, and I needed something fast. I tried again in the government but everything seemed to get back to the civil service rigmarole, and going that route would take forever. I went to a career counselor who told me about networking, and I soon became a "networker," but Betsy was giving me a hard time about typing letters after six o'clock at night, this being the era before electronic word processing. And in any case, anyone who has ever landed anything by networking knows that it can take time, and time was not on my side.

At this point the guy who had originally told me about the writing job for the government said he knew a general contractor who needed a laborer and would pay me $4 an hour. I signed on. I had worked for my cousin as a housepainter for two summers as a teenager, so I was at least familiar with the building trades. I didn't have to join a union or anything, and after having spent years in school, there was something very fitting, very Zen, very politically correct, about working with my hands instead of my brain, my back instead of my mouth. The weather was perfect to be outdoors, I was drinking Schlitz beer out of a can instead of cappuccino in cafés, and it felt good to be earning money in work that was more enjoyable than I thought it would be, even though Bill, my boss, was totally disorganized, which led to an irregular job schedule. But at least I was pulling down about a hundred bucks a week, and my self-esteem was gradually reemerging.

My new gig had no effect on Betsy. She was contemptuous of the work and the guys who did it, and she let me know that she didn't consider it a proper career for someone with a Ph.D. She insisted that I get my own apartment. That would be the only way we could evaluate what was left between us. It was just too stressful to have me around. I continued to "network" on the days I didn't work construction, tried to type cover and thank you letters before "the dinner hour," and thought a lot about who I was professionally.

For a man in contemporary society, there is no greater consideration. The roles of father, son, brother, husband, and friend pale in comparison to the significance most men place on what they do in the world. It represents the hierarchy, the pecking order, the status that men have traditionally employed to compete with one another for the most desirable women, the greatest perks and privileges, earnings and other forms of financial rewards, power, and in some rare cases, fame and fortune. Men willingly sacrifice all else for career. When people meet for the first time they ask "What is your name?" and then "What do you do?"

When the universe was giving men the ability to define themselves by the work they did, I must have been elsewhere, because I don't have it, never did, and probably never will. It's almost as if I'm missing a gene. Before I was ten I wanted to be a ballplayer. From ten to fifteen, it was a meteorologist. When I looked back recently in my high school yearbook and saw that I had listed my intended career as medicine, I laughed and presumed it was a mistake until I remembered that for a week in eleventh grade I wanted to be a psychiatrist. Then for a few years it was a lawyer, but not because I really wanted to argue criminal cases like Perry Mason, but because I fancied myself a budding politician and all successful politicians then were lawyers.

When the sixties hit, I had a rationalization for my inability to identify a career path. I no longer had any desire to do anything that required a jacket and tie, so law and politics were both out. I then got caught up in the draft quagmire and would have been content to teach elementary school for the rest of my life, but if it didn't keep me out of Vietnam, I had no attachment to that, either. I started graduate school with the idea of becoming like Dr. Weber, a college history teacher who was a true inspiration, but I was prepared to leave academia and work for George McGovern—which I did—and go to Washington in the unlikely event that he won. When he didn't, I got my Ph.D. but then couldn't find a full-time job in academia.

Betsy was making me pay part of her rent, and so I couldn't seem to accumulate enough money to get a place of my own, a catch-22 if I ever heard of one. My net worth was now down to $500 and I was considering my only other option—calling my parents in Philadelphia and asking them for money, something

I was loath to do. This was distasteful to me not because there was a chance that they would refuse, since there wasn't, but because I would have to explain myself to them, tell them what I was doing, what my plans were, why I was in Washington living with that shiksa and pouring concrete in the hot sun when I had just spent years studying for that meshuga Ph.D., and now I wasn't even doing anything with it. I would have had to endure my mother saying to me for the six thousandth time that I should have been a lawyer, and that would have been almost unendurable. For the truth was that I couldn't explain myself, at least not to them, for they spent forty-four years in the same business before retiring.

I felt stuck, trapped, and I wanted to go back to New York, back to playing boxball, back to the snowstorm when I walked home. I wanted to crawl back into the womb. Life was unfriendly, hostile, frustrating, and all because I was a man, had no money, and didn't know what to do to earn enough on my own. Robbing a bank or running marijuana were out of the question, and selling insurance door to door probably wouldn't pay off. I needed a miracle.

Most people have a notion of miracles that is directly out of the Bible—or a Cecil B. DeMille movie version of the Bible. In my case, an unexpected encounter turned out to be the miracle I was fervently praying for.

I was sitting in Betsy's car not far from the Washington Hilton Hotel when a man whom I hadn't seen in about ten years but whom I immediately recognized, Howard Davis, walked by. He was a high school classmate with whom I had also shared a freshman English class in college, and I hadn't seen him since then. He looked the same but had lost his hair, and when I called out his name he immediately turned around, approached the car, and asked if he knew me.

I said that he did, and when I identified myself, he of course remembered, apologizing for the temporary lapse.

"Alan Epstein, my God, I would never have recognized you. For one thing, you have so much hair—and a beard."

"Yeah, well, none of us had beards at Central."

"It looks great on you. And you're so much thinner than the last time I saw you."

"I don't eat meat anymore."

He rolled his eyes. "Oh, one of those. Well, enough of this. How are you?"

"I'm fine, Howard," I answered. "How are you?"

"Going crazy," he said, shaking his head and letting out a very deep sigh. "I just bought this beautiful five-room co-op not far from here, but it needs work, especially painting, and I'm going nuts trying to figure out who to hire. I've already talked to about five contractors."

I was listening so carefully I thought he would be able to see my eyes bulging and my ears twitching, as I strained to hear him correctly. "What's the problem?" I asked.

"Only that I can't decide. They're all so, you know, blue-collar. As I said, I just bought this place, and I really want it to come out right."

Now my heart was racing with excitement. All the years of study, of application, of intense focus on trying to uncover the meaning of almost everything came down to a single moment in time when more than anything else the meaning of *my* life was that I needed money. I decided to go for the jugular. "Howard, listen, you can stop thinking about it. Your problem is solved."

"What do you mean?" he asked, quizzically.

"I'll do it."

"You! You're a housepainter?"

"You got it. I just moved here from New York. It's a very long story, which I'll tell you someday. But I've been here for about two months trying to get it together after getting my Ph.D. at NYU, and right now I'm supporting myself working construction."

"You're kidding. I never would have guessed. The last time I saw you, we were reading Dickens, and here it is ten years later and you want to paint my co-op."

"Life's strange, isn't it, Howard. When can I start?"

"Whoa, wait a minute. I like this idea, but how much would you charge?"

Now I was stumped. I had no idea how much work was involved, no equipment, no guarantee that Bill would give me the time off, and no one to help me. But somehow I knew that the opportunity was at hand, and that telling him that I would get back to him, or that I needed time to figure it out, or that I would have to put together an estimate, I would lose him. I have spent enough subsequent years in sales to know that people may persuade themselves rationally to move toward buying something, but that the actual decision is often an impulsive one, basically a leap of faith.

"What's your lowest bid?" I ventured, suddenly knowing what to say only when the words spilled out of my mouth.

"It's $875, and that's for two coats—color—and the trim."

"Fine, I'll do it for $850."

"You will? This is great," he said. "I can't believe this. Five minutes ago I was walking around trying to figure out what to do, and then I run into someone I haven't seen in ten years and he's going to paint my apartment."

"As I've already said, Howard, life is strange. Anything is possible."

"Didn't Mr. Barrett say that at Central?"

"Hmm, I thought it was Buddha."

"Well, anyway, somehow I get the feeling that I can trust you more than the other painters." He put out his hand, which I shook. He then wrote down his phone number. "Call me and I'll show you the place. I need the work done two weeks from now. Is that okay with you?"

"That's fine, Howard. Thanks so much. You have no idea what this means to me."

"Don't mention it. I feel really good about this."

"So do I. By the way, what do you do?"

"I'm a lawyer with the Department of Labor. It's pretty boring, but it's a job."

"I'd like to hear about it sometime," I said, working hard to suppress a smile, thinking that very easily that could have been me. "Thanks, Howard. I'll be in touch."

Who needed Charlton Heston when I had Howard? I had already looked at an apartment that suited me, but it had been difficult to commit to it with my finances in such shaky condition. But now I had work for which I would be paid $850, and after I figured out my expenses, I would certainly have more money than I had been earning since I left New York.

I called my brother, Perry, in Philadelphia and asked if he would come down to help me. I had been around house-painting enough to know that the job would require two people for one week. If I paid Perry $4 an hour—as Bill was paying me—and the work took as long as I anticipated, then he would get about $150, leaving me with $700. Then there was the matter of paint and supplies. After I saw Howard's place, which looked like it hadn't been coated in twenty-five years, Bill helped me figure out how much paint I would need, and then went with me to buy it. I dipped into my savings, which were rapidly approaching zero, and took out $225 to buy the paint, rollers, brushes, and pans needed to do the job right. Bill said he would lend me some drop cloths, and that I could take the week off to do the job.

I signed the lease on the apartment, leaving me with about $25 to my name. I had never had so little money. There was always the phone call I could make to Philadelphia, but I wanted to avoid that if I could. The next few weeks would be critical. Bill said there was a house he was going to build— a big house—in Potomac, Maryland, not far from D.C., and when that started, which should be at the end of August, it would mean steady work for months. Bill was just as much on the edge as I was, but at least he owned his own house, had a truck, and his mother, with whom he lived, bought groceries and cooked for him. He was the most disorganized person I had ever met, but he was also sweet and generous, and his favorite line was that the morning's second cup of coffee was better than the first, which he repeated every few days.

I moved into my place, which to no great surprise improved relations with Betsy. She came over during her lunch break the first day, and we inaugurated the place by making love on the living-room floor between piles of books. We had already officially "broken up," which meant to Betsy that she wasn't in love with me anymore, but that didn't seem to have had a harmful effect on her libido, which in fact seemed more intact than it had been at any time since the beginning of our relationship. But by this time I knew it was not meant to be with Betsy.

Getting my own place did wonders for me in other ways. I could type after six o'clock in the evening. I liked the Dupont Circle area much more than the somewhat snooty atmosphere of Georgetown, and I once again had the opportunity—living alone—to collect myself, gather my thoughts, discover who I was and what I wanted, without the critical eye of Betsy, who, when she wasn't interested in sex, had turned into something of a shrew. Now we could "date" again, see each other when we wanted to, not because we had to, and it became an arrangement that worked out better for both of us.

Perry came down and helped me paint Howard's apartment. Everything went according to plan. The supplies I bought were the ones I needed, we had enough paint, and Howard, who to my surprise turned out to be gay, loved the way the colors he chose looked on the walls. Bill even helped, plastering up a section of the hall ceiling, where an electrician had put in track lighting. Bill didn't charge me anything, saying he wanted this job to be finished as soon as possible because right after he said he could spare me to paint the co-op, a lot of work came in for him, and he needed to get to it before we started on the big house in Potomac.

Perry and I had a blast painting, even though the weather was oppressively hot. It was one of the longest heat waves in memory, with temperatures climbing above ninety degrees for twenty-one days in a row. Combined with the chronic summer humidity, which was much worse than anything I had experienced in either Philadelphia or New York, we had to do whatever we could to stay cool, which meant drinking a lot of beer. I paid Perry his $150, which angered my mother, who said he should have done it for free because he was my brother. She insisted that he give it back to me. Since he lived at home he didn't need it was how she thought, but I said he had earned it, and I wanted him to keep it.

As for me, at the end of the week I had $475 more dollars in my pocket than I did at the beginning, and the prospect of steady work, which would amount to about $640 per month, meant I could easily afford to pay my $240 rent. I had no car, no health insurance, no debts, and no girlfriend, which in 1977 meant that I would be able to maintain my household on the $400 left over each month, and in fact I did.

Things began to work out beautifully. I did spend that entire fall working on the house in Potomac. The weather finally cooled off in September and for weeks it felt great to be out every day in the fine, fresh autumn air. I was in great shape, learned to walk on floor joists ten feet above the ground, and saw how a house goes up, from the foundation to the roof.

It was a great experience, as were the other jobs I worked on with Bill: converting a basement into an apartment, enclosing a patio to make a den, and renovating an old structure to turn it into a town house. I learned all about tools, how each individual task requires the right one, how to organize a job, how plumbing relates to dry wall, framing to electrical, rough work to finish work, and so on, and had great philosophical discussions with the tradesmen I met on each of these jobs, who were much more enlightened politically than anyone in academia would ever have imagined.

But when I look back at that time, it was that serendipitous meeting with Howard Davis that triggered the positive chain of events. When things turn around, as any terrible situation inevitably must, there is usually one event, one occurrence, that in retrospect started the change of luck. One of the greatest philosophers of the twentieth century, Mick Jagger, said it best: "You can't always get what you want . . . but if you try sometime, you get what you need." Amen.

The only sour note during the week Perry and I painted was that Elvis died, but I haven't been able to this day to determine if there was any connection between that sad and unexpected event and the fact that I had moved to Washington, didn't get a job I thought I had, was kicked out of Betsy's place, ran into Howard Davis after ten years, painted his co-op, and earned enough money to get my own place and my feet on the ground. Maybe someday I'll figure it all out.

From the vantage point of twenty years later, it is easy to look back at this time and be thankful for the opportunity to learn a lesson about life—that random events do conspire to turn situations around. Having gone through this experience, I was well prepared the next time it happened, and the next time after that, because in fact this is what navigating through life is all about. Having come from a family where the members wanted everything to be *known,* I have had to learn about dealing with what cannot by definition be known—the future.

The other major discovery was about resourcefulness. I grew up thinking in institutional terms, that family, school, and ultimately some organization would take care of me forever. But that has not turned out to be the case. I have had on more than one occasion to fall back on my wiles, to take lemons and make lemonade, and this comes from being able to think "outside the box," as today's parlance would have it. To take advantage of opportunities, to know when to move and when to hold back, with whom to associate, to understand the difference between a helping hand and something more permanent, all come from living each day as if life were one grand school, one that continually affords the possibility of knowing that there is so much more to it than the five-year plan. Which is not to say that one shouldn't have one, but which is to say that it should be ready to be thrown out if other circumstances arise.

8

A Date

with Death

EVEN THE SIMPLEST activities can be
fraught with danger. Think about the ordinary act of cutting
a bagel for your breakfast or stepping out of the tub after a
long, leisurely bath. If your attention slips and the knife slides
off the bagel, your next stop may be the emergency room of
the local hospital. And if you're not careful about how you
come out of the tub, you could easily lose your balance and
fall. The line between health and sickness, safety and mishap,
painlessness and injury is indeed a thin one, and we skirt it
every day when we perform the ordinary act of getting behind
the wheels of our cars.

In retrospect, rolling into Zimmerman's garage door as a
virgin driver was something to laugh about, mostly because no
one was hurt. It was a unique way in which to initiate myself
into the world of driving. The fact that the incident forced me
to have an encounter with my own moral compass only served
to make the mishap that much more memorable. But driving

a car is a dangerous, risky venture; at any moment one can suddenly be confronted with a life and death situation. It happens every day all over the world. And for many, the result is injury, often serious injury, and sometimes even worse than that.

My own experience with driving has been an ironic one. After all the years of longing for the freedom that driving brings, I moved to New York City in 1971, six years after I obtained my license, and did not take a car. I was delighted to have the opportunity to dispose of my vehicle and become a patron of public transportation. Buses, subways, and trains became my reality, and it was seven years before I was forced to own another vehicle, having moved out of New York and back into "America." Living in San Francisco three years later, I found myself driving my '78 Honda Civic—a decidedly small car, dubbed The Tomato—home after a day spent visiting with friends from the East Coast who were staying in a downtown hotel.

It was shortly after midnight on a Saturday night as I made my way south on U.S. 101 in San Francisco, about to exit at Army Street to drive the last ten minutes to my apartment. I was already beginning to think about the next day, a barbecue in Berkeley that I was looking forward to, as there would be some friends at the party that I had not seen in a while. The solstice had just occurred a few days before and summer in the Bay Area had arrived, not the warmest time but certainly warm enough. I was also reminiscing about the hours I had just spent with my old buddy Steve Brown, who had been instrumental in getting my "career" launched in construction as a resident of the nation's capital. But my heart had always been left in San Francisco, and when I had an opportunity to live there, I took advantage of it and moved as far west as one can go and still remain in the continental United States. I was finally a Californian.

U.S. 101 was relatively quiet as the minutes ticked by and the Army Street exit approached. I was in the lane next to the far right one and was about to make my way right to prepare to exit when I noticed a car pass me two lanes to my left, in the far left lane, at breakneck speed. The car could easily have been going 100 miles per hour. And it was not moving in a straight line either, but rather swerving precariously between two lanes. I made a mental note to stay as far away as I could, which wasn't much of a problem since at the speed I was traveling there was no way I could catch up. I signaled right to move over and off the highway. As I watched his taillights become smaller in the distance, I felt reassured that I would soon be off the freeway and onto the familiar streets of my Noe Valley neighborhood. I would be asleep in fifteen minutes, or as soon as I laid my head on my pillow.

I was now in the right lane and approaching the last overpass before I would exit. Perhaps five seconds had elapsed since the speeding car had passed me. I had one eye on the exit and the other on the car when suddenly I was plowed into and pushed off the road by a much bigger vehicle that had come across the freeway at a forty-five degree angle and hit the front end of my car, just in front of the driver's door. Whereas seconds before I was thinking about restful sleep, having had a pleasant day that lasted past midnight, now I was struggling to maintain control of the steering wheel, as I was no longer traveling in the direction I wanted to go. The force of the impact had knocked me out of my lane and onto the shoulder of the road, and directly in front of me and looming fast was the concrete face of a wall that supported the overpass above. There was no way I could stop myself from hitting it, and in such a small car, the odds were that the Honda would collapse like an accordion and I would be crushed against the engine.

So this is how I am going to die. That was what immediately came to mind. How common, how ordinary, how banal, to have one's life end on a highway in California at one o'clock in the morning on a Saturday night. I was about to become a statistic, just one more digit in the mounting number of unfortunate souls who lost their bodies somewhere out on the road. Death was approaching. In the confusion and terror of what I was suddenly experiencing, the only thing that was clear to me, that was certain, was that I unexpectedly had a date with death, that the speed and direction of my tiny vehicle and the fact that I was about to meet the immense implacability of the concrete wall would combine to erase Alan Epstein forever. I had no idea what was to come next, but in a way I began to relax and surrender myself to my fate, which I was powerless to overcome.

Imagine my shock when I hit the wall and was immediately aware that I was not only still alive but as yet felt no pain, that somehow The Tomato had absorbed the impact and not given ground to the wall. Although I had survived so far, I was nowhere near out of danger, as I was now moving backward from the impact and spinning wildly. But there was no mistaking the fact that a very important change had taken place inside of me in the intervening few seconds. Because I had survived the first contact, with the other car, and the second impact, with the wall, there came upon me the recognition that giving up now would be foolish, that there was a life and death situation to manage and that there was absolutely no certainty that I was about to die. I resolved that if that eventuality were to befall me, it would be only after a struggle.

My hands were still firmly on the wheel, I was not injured as far as I could tell, and if I did not roll over, which was a distinct possibility, I might survive the unfortunate incident that had materialized. The moment of resignation had passed, and the part of me that had gotten Jim Brown's autograph eighteen years earlier had now taken over. I still had a long way to go and I was not going to die on a highway alone. Although there is obviously only so much one can do in a situation like this, and things are happening so fast that one is doing well just to keep one's wits together, there is still the choice to be the warrior, to be the one who can stare death in the face without blinking and perhaps make it go away simply because death knows the struggle will not be an easy one.

This is perhaps the most interesting thing about death: because we know nothing about it—at least nothing we can count on—it lends itself marvelously to speculation. Death is nothing if not possibility, and I choose to believe that it is an entity, something of nature that has consciousness and exists everywhere. It was paying me a visit that June night in San Francisco, and there was no doubt that it was trying to see if it could take me with it, wherever it was going. It's just that I didn't want to go, and that meant managing the situation to minimize the possibility that death would prevail. And so when it was apparent to me that my car was not turning over, that I would continue to spin without toppling, I experienced a kind of elation that must be what politicians feel after they've won an election.

I had dodged another bullet, the third so far, but I was not in the clear because the impact of the wall had pushed me back into the right lane of the freeway, and I could be hit again, which was a distinct possibility, since it was Saturday night and vehicles would be coming south on 101 at high speeds, not expecting to see a car spinning like a top in the right lane. Something was telling me that I had run out of chances, and that if death were to throw out another thunderbolt, say in the form of being hit by a speeding vehicle while I was spinning, that somehow I was not going to survive another crash, that the sheer physics of the situation would be working against me. Please God, please if it is in fact you who helps us mortals cheat death, if you are the one with ultimate say in these matters, please God, please don't let another car come by and plow into me. Things are bad enough in here without having to deal with something else.

But the fear of being struck again was immediately replaced with a counterthought, precisely the process that had been going on all along—thought, counterthought, thought, counterthought—that if I were going to be snatched unceremoniously from this particular lifetime in this particular manner, then it would have happened already, and because it hadn't so far, my fear evaporated in the next instant, and I was back trying to make sure I didn't make any false moves. And so when I finally came to a halt after pretending to be a dreidel for a few agonizingly long seconds, I wasn't even surprised when I realized that I had not been hit. Death had had its chance, and either I or God or some other force had fought it off. Or maybe all this stuff about death is silly and I was just lucky to be alive, that fate had decreed it wasn't quite my time.

The next sight snapped me out of my reverie. The Tomato had stopped in the extreme right lane, facing across the freeway. To my left, in each of the four lanes, were cars, lined up in a neat row as if they were stopped for an ordinary traffic light. They had come upon the chaos that was me and my car and stopped in time. It was only then, when I realized that I had indeed survived this encounter with the other side, that my body allowed itself, completely involuntarily, to experience the full weight of what had just taken place. In a moment I was transfixed, paralyzed with fear, and could do nothing but stare at the vehicles lined up on Highway 101, waiting so patiently. I had survived, as far as I could tell I wasn't hurt, and just thirty seconds or so had elapsed between the time I saw the first speeding car and now.

Out of the darkness came a man, seemingly from nowhere, whom I quickly gleaned was the driver of the other vehicle. He said in broken English that his car was still drivable but that his girlfriend was hurt. Since San Francisco General Hospital was moments from where the accident had taken place, he would drive us there to get help. I got out of the Honda, which he helped push onto the shoulder of the road, since the front end has been smashed in. We ran to his car, where I encountered a woman bleeding from the head, moaning in obvious pain, and holding on to her arm. Within minutes we were in the emergency room, where she was whisked off and I was left to review whatever injuries I had with a solicitous nurse, but not before I had a chance to ask the other guy what happened. Whether he was purposefully evasive or truly ignorant I'll never know, but he vaguely mentioned the first car, and I could not tell whether he in fact knew the other driver or was trying to get out of the way himself. I spoke briefly with the highway patrolman who took down the pertinent information, and it was he who informed me that the other driver was legally over the limit as far as alcohol was concerned, and that if I could avoid it in the future, I should stay off the roads on Saturday night because most of the drivers out at that time were DWI. He also told me that the overwhelming number of fatalities on the road involved drunken driving and that I should consider myself to be very lucky, as if I needed him to tell me so.

I never saw or spoke to the other driver again, and never found out anything more about what happened that night. What mattered at that point was that I had not been killed or even injured in what was by anyone's standards a major car accident, my first imbroglio since Zimmerman's garage door years before, and the first time I had experienced the terror of feeling like a pinball at 55 miles per hour.

I called a tow truck to help deal with the smashed Tomato. It was only then, in the deep dark dead of night, that I realized what a yeoman job my little Honda Civic had done. For there, perhaps 100 feet up the road from the point of the collision, was my front bumper, which absorbed the full impact of the wall. On the car itself are two metal struts that hold the bumper about six inches in front of the body, and these small metal supports were bent back and actually touching the body. Had they buckled on impact, which was what I was fully expecting them to do, I would have been a dead man.

I threw the bumper in the car and rode home in the tow truck, arriving at 2:30 A.M. I felt as though I had just run a marathon. My ears were ringing, and the silence of the middle of the night was loud and eerie. When I slipped under the covers and put my head down, it occurred to me suddenly how soft my bed was, that I had just spent a few moments in a cold, hard world, a world of steel, glass, and concrete, of sharp edges. To lie in a comfortable, familiar place was a gift beyond expectation, and to my surprise I fell asleep instantly.

When I awoke the next morning I experienced for the first time in my life what it meant on the most elementary level to have a body, because it hurt bad. Every square inch of bone, muscle, and organ was sore, as if I had gone ten rounds with Mike Tyson and he had been able to pound me wherever he wanted. This was the aftermath of shock, when my body was forced to recognize that it had undergone something so extraordinary, so beyond its usual capabilities, that what it longed for more than anything was a chance to relax, and making me hurt was its way of saying that I was not to engage in anything more strenuous than fixing a cup of tea. But by noontime the ache had subsided considerably, and, without the use of a vehicle for the first time since my New York days, I set out in the manner to which people had grown accustomed before the arrival of the internal combustion engine—by foot.

The three-mile hike to downtown San Francisco was one of the most exhilarating experiences I have ever had—before or since. To breathe in the incomparably fresh Bay Area air, to watch the faces of strangers, to become aware of one's body all combined to create a feeling of excitement and peacefulness at the same time. It would have been impossible for anyone to tell from the satisfied look with which I went through that day that just hours before my life had been seriously jeopardized, and that I had escaped injury for reasons I and no one else will ever know. If it hadn't been for the wreck of my car standing forlornly in my garage, waiting to be picked up so that it could be put back together again, I might have blocked out the memory of the night before, not wanting to believe that life could be so calm and uneventful one moment, so horrifying the next, and back again, all in the space of a relatively small period of time. If one is fortunate and manages to survive such an accident intact, what is often left is a sense of having just had an encounter with something truly extraordinary, and this can teach us more in a few moments than some experiences can in a lifetime or two. The knowledge of the immediacy of death is really what enables us to live fully in the present.

9

Big Boys
Do Cry

OPERA IS DEFINITELY an acquired taste, especially for Americans, who usually find the entire enterprise incomprehensible—those outlandish costumes and sets, the intolerable length, the exorbitant prices, and those languages! But for me it certainly has been a taste worth acquiring. In fact, there was a moment in my life when listening to Italian opera led me into a deep emotional catharsis that I had no idea I was desperately in need of, when the music and the meaning worked on my soul to release feelings that had remained locked away for a very long time.

My own contact with opera began almost imperceptibly. As I sat in a movie theater one day watching a very underrated British film called *Sunday, Bloody, Sunday*, I became intoxicated by a musical refrain that surfaced over and over during the film, notes that I had never heard before, a sonorous, heavenly sound that captured the attention of my entire being every time I heard it, and heard it often I did.

This particular piece of music was as central to the movie as "We're Off to See the Wizard" is to Dorothy and her companions, and each time I heard it, I felt a tingling throughout my nervous system that produced one of the most relaxed feelings of well-being that I had ever experienced.

As the movie ended I sat anxiously through the interminable scroll of credits to find out what in the name of God I had just heard. And then it came on. I knew it wasn't Duke Ellington, so it had to be the aria "Soave sia il vento" (May the Wind Be Gentle) from Mozart's comic opera *Così fan tutte.* I had of course heard of Mozart, but not of this particular piece, and so I made a beeline from the theater to a record store to make sure that I could listen to these notes whenever I wanted.

For days I sat in the living room of my apartment and listened to those arching sopranos reach so far into the upper registers of their voices that I could have sworn that they were no longer human but sounds that one would undoubtedly hear if one could actually visit heaven. If this was opera, how could I stop myself from hearing more?

I had always loved music as a child and then as a teenager, listening constantly to the Top 40 and then to rock. After that I branched out into jazz and classical, but opera remained a foreign language. I knew who Luciano Pavarotti was, but beyond that, my ignorance was almost complete. I could not name a single opera except for the most obvious ones like *Carmen*, *Rigoletto*, and *La Bohème*, knew nothing of the composers, and remained far outside the operatic world.

I had to start somewhere, and so my next stop was to see a performance of Verdi's *La Traviata* at the Kennedy Center in

Washington, where I was living at the time. I got hold of a recording of the opera before I went to the theater and tried to listen to it as many times as I could, but I was decidedly unmoved as I sat in the audience for three and a half hours, wondering why I wasn't enjoying what I was hearing. I couldn't of course understand what they were singing, and although the music was technically correct, as far as I could tell, nothing in the performance spoke to me. It was not my beloved "Soave sia il vento," and the critical thinking part of me was saying that just because I found one aria that I loved didn't mean I was going to become an opera buff. And so for years, that one aria from that one opera was it for me, but every time I heard the soft strings introduce what I knew would follow, it was like an invitation to drop whatever I was doing and experience the feeling of immortality. All I could think of was paradise. The music said to me, "Yes, there is a heaven, and this is what it sounds like." And if that were the case, then whatever happened in life could be endured because the possibility of being in the place that the music conjured up was always there. It had to be, or else the music wouldn't exist. I didn't know if I had to die to get there, but if I did, then maybe death wasn't so bad.

The music of course was beautiful, but there was obviously something in me that longed for a life that was calm, still, and painless. What the music did—aside from being technically sublime—was act as a catalyst to set off these feelings within me. I began to realize that I was not a very happy person, that the music was a salve, an emotional crutch on which I could rest the unhappy psychology with which life had saddled me. The reasons for my discontent were complicated and personal, but suffice it to say that listening over and over again to that aria began to stir up inside me deep feelings of disappointment, of heartache, and it got to the point where I could not listen to the music without immediately getting that sense of leaving behind my earthly cares and entering a dimension in which I didn't want or need anything or anyone.

Guided by a friend whose knowledge of the art form was as deep as his appreciation, and aided by a music store nearby that sold used recordings at ludicrously low prices, I then plunged without reservation into the world of opera. I exposed myself to different eras, composers, languages, and artists, beginning at the same time to become emotionally sensitized to the failures and disappointments I had experienced in this lifetime. Although I had a Ph.D., I had no noticeable career at thirty-three years of age, and had a broken marriage. The more I listened to opera, the more I got in touch with that sadness, that disappointment, that sense of failure. Why had my marriage not worked? Why hadn't I been able to find another partner in the eight years since Judy and I divorced? Why had every single one of my intimate relationships in the intervening time ended painfully? Why was I so alone? Why hadn't I been able to find a place for myself, my "spot," as Don Juan called it? My career was no career. I had had a series of jobs that called upon me to perform a variety of tasks, but none had truly satisfied me. What was this all about? Where did I fit? Who was I? All this knowledge, all this intelligence, all this potential, and I was still unable to put it together into a life package that would suit my ambition.

As these questions began to dominate my existence, as I started to spend more time alone to ponder the meaning and purpose of my existence, the music of opera began to speak to me in a way I had never experienced. All the books I had read on psychology, philosophy, religion, or science seemed trivial in the face of a few musical bars strung together in such a way as to render me speechless and emotionally vulnerable.

It is an old saw in philosophical lore than when the pupil is ready, the teacher will appear. Five years after first hearing Mozart's haunting melody, I taped from the radio the 1982 performance of Opera in the Park—a San Francisco tradition that kicks off the fall season each year. It is usually a collection of crowd pleasers, and included in that year's selections were two tenor arias, "É lucevan le stelle," from Puccini's *Tosca*, and "Vesti la giubba," from Leoncavallo's *Pagliacci*.

They might have been familiar to others, but they weren't to me, and when I began to listen to these arias, and grasp their meaning, they unleashed a flood of emotion that I wasn't aware I was capable of. The music is powerful and compelling, but the stories behind the notes filled in the blanks and served to push me emotionally over the edge. In *Tosca*, Cavaradossi sings passionately that he is about to be executed by the authority of a very evil man, and the irony of his impending death is not lost on him—just when, for the first time in his life, he has found love ("E non ho amato mai tanto la vita" [And Never Before Have I Loved Life So Much]). In *Pagliacci*, Tonio the clown is getting ready to go out and make people laugh, even though his heart is broken as a result of learning that his wife has betrayed him.

There was something about the irony of these two situations, the tragedy, the humanness, that took me not to the heaven of Mozart but into the hell that was my own emotional life. The pain of Mario Cavaradossi and Tonio the clown became my pain, their struggles to contend with their misfortunes my misfortune, the threat to their masculinity a threat to my masculinity, and all I could do was listen to their beautiful, painful wailing, to their crying out to God in heaven to find out why they had been dealt with so unjustly, and feel every ounce of sadness I had ever felt in my own life or in the lives of anyone I had ever known personally or read about. The horrors of history, the brutality of one person's behavior toward another, the knowledge that as humans we are made of the stuff of both angels and devils was too much to hold in, and I began to weep as soon as I heard their plaintive voices, in a way that I probably had not sobbed since I was a baby.

I could not stop crying. I could not keep the tears from coming. The emotional catharsis of wailing into handkerchief after handkerchief became a sort of addiction that I could not get enough of, so satisfying, so wonderful, so intoxicating was the feeling I was experiencing every time I heard the voices and began to sob. I was crying for all men and women who had ever suffered, who had been treated unfairly, for all those who deserved a better fate. But I was crying as well for all my sufferings, for every time I had been treated unfairly, for those moments when I too deserved something other than what life had dealt me.

Deepak Chopra says that tears of happiness have a different biochemistry from tears of sorrow. What then of the biochemistry of tears of neither joy nor sorrow, but of simply being human, of the sheer immensity of the proposition that I am both who I am and also of the same stuff as everyone else? What is the composition of the tears of existence, of existential tears, of the knowledge that I and others are capable of feeling such a wide range of emotions that it is literally impossible to catalogue them all.

Weeping became my little secret. When others were out food-shopping, watching *Wheel of Fortune* on television, talking to their boyfriends on the telephone, or yelling at their stockbrokers for some less than profitable investments, I was sitting alone in my living room, crying my eyes out day after day to music that I had listened to for years but that had never before affected me so. There were times when I thought the spell was over, when I would sit and listen and nothing would happen other than deep appreciation for the artistry of Puccini, and I would sigh with relief that I could resume normal life; then in a flash a certain note would be reached and the dam would break again and I was forced to relive the emotional catharsis one more time. And once I got rolling I could not stop.

There was no doubt that the accumulated weeping was having a salutary effect on me, and that I felt great at the end of each bout. My entire body felt cleansed of everything that had ever disappointed me or made me suffer. I was in the process of ameliorating all the times I had loved and lost, every instance where someone's careless remark or behavior had caused me pain, all the myriad slights and slurs that every human being must endure in the course of his or her life. Everything was coming up and out, occasioned by the simple relationships between sounds and nothingness that is what music really is, and how these particular arrangements can affect us emotionally in ways that are unexpected and uncontrollable.

What was also not lost on me was the fact that I am male, and that from a very early age, from as far back as we can remember, we are taught in this most unemotional Anglo-Saxon culture of ours not to express our feelings if we want to be real men, that big boys don't cry. We are taught to hold back, to suffer in silence, to repress that part of us that is just screaming in pain, the inevitable pain we must feel from time to time as humans. After a while we men, we warriors, we tough guys don't have any feelings at all. And this is what our culture actually wants from us, for how else would we be able to go about the dirty work of society, of killing in wars, of ferocious acts of bravery, of going up against the best the other company has to offer and getting the contract anyway, if we weren't taught not to cry, not to hold back our feelings, not to pretend that everything is OK when it isn't.

To do what I was doing was my choice. I could have gone to the gym and shot hoops, or stayed later at work and made five more calls. I could have put on the jarring chaos of The Pretenders instead of Puccini, listened to cool Miles Davis instead of Giordano, but that would have been so far off the mark at that particular point in my life that I wouldn't have lasted thirty seconds without returning to what I needed. What forced those salty tears up and out of my eyes was the varied notes of the human drama, as interpreted by Italian composers, themselves steeped in a culture that knows how to emote, that doesn't hold back when it comes to feelings—joys or sorrows, triumphs or tragedies. And I'm talking about the men as well.

But then I was to learn that I wasn't finished, that my encounter with something deep, something personal, something wild and unfinished within had not yet run its course. It was after I had exhausted the pathos of Cavaradossi and Tonio that I discovered the female side of the tragedy, the soprano side. I heard Puccini's heroines sing their hearts out for me, and I responded once again to the lilting notes of the soprano voice that truly is an instrument in itself. In particular the arias that touched me were Mimi's introduction of herself to Rodolfo in *La Bohème*, when, after explaining that she has nothing materially to speak of, she nevertheless is powerfully moved by the appearance of the warm sun in springtime, and the poignant "Un bel di" of *Madama Butterfly*, Cio-Cio-San, the Japanese waif who naively believes that her American officer husband's return is imminent. In the aria, she describes in glorious detail his arrival, and how she will greet him.

What is so touching, so compelling, so dramatic about both these arias is that we all know that the lieutenant isn't coming back, and that Mimi is in fact dying of consumption. It is precisely this human capability to hold on to hope in the face of crushing defeat that so moves us, and when I began to fully imbibe the meaning of what I was listening to, I began again to feel the suffering associated with dashed expectations—my own included—and I was plunged once more into an emotional abyss that if anything was deeper than the previous one.

Was it the fact that I was listening to the voices of women carrying me to these deeper places? Listening to these two arias made Cavaradossi's and Tonio's struggles seem trivial by comparison. Is tragedy in women that much more tragic? The female voice an instrument more suitable to getting at the innermost emotional recesses in both men and women? Was the genius of Puccini to realize this and put those powerful notes in the soprano voice?

In the midst of the emotional chasm that had opened in my life I tried to bring friends along with me to the world I was going to at every opportunity, but I soon realized that it was too personal. It wasn't really the music that was making me cry *but my relationship to the music,* and this was so wrapped up in my own recesses that it could not be translated into anyone else's emotional language. It pained me to sit with someone else, listening to Mimi hit the highest notes, and basically watch my friend smile bravely to indicate that it was a good performance. I knew I was on this road alone and that I would have to travel the length of it without assistance. As long as I felt the need to get in touch with something inside me that had not been resolved, I could put on an opera recording and sob away to my heart's content. And given the buckets of tears I shed in that two-week period in the fall of 1982, when I was confronting the various hopes that in my life had been dashed, I was thankful that there came along at a time when I really needed it a vehicle to release my anger, my frustration, my sadness and sorrow in a relatively healthy manner. If every man or woman sat in his or her living room and cried cathartic tears every time he or she felt a deep, deep pain, then the world would be a calmer, saner, less threatening place.

There was something else to that bout of temporary madness, or what seems like madness compared to what is considered normal behavior for a fully functioning adult male. Part of what I was crying about was to acknowledge, through all the sorrow, all the pain, the utter and absolute perfection of human existence. These composers, people of flesh and blood, who were of course subject to the same emotional confrontations as the characters they created and inspired, were capable of rendering the full panoply of human experience in such a profoundly moving and artful way. Although the situations were all about pain and suffering, the way in which their stories were presented to the human ear, the joy that is experienced as a result of the music, gives lie to the pain, and indicates, once again through the medium of art, that the human spirit is indomitable, that its destiny is to triumph over tragedy, even if it can do so only by turning the agony of suffering into something beautiful for someone else to appreciate.

This is also why it is so difficult to deal with emotions, with one's own and with those of others. They are too complex to respond to easy remedies. There is too much that is interconnected to lend themselves to quick solutions. I am reminded of Rilke's remark that he resisted psychoanalysis because he feared that it would exorcise his angels along with his demons. Perhaps it would have helped to listen to Puccini.

10

New York

Story

H OW DOES ONE balance the need to take
risks in love with the desire not to be hurt? Can one have one
without the other? As in other areas of life, where there is no
risk there is no reward. But as also so often happens in life, the
results of risk are mixed.

My own philosophy when it came to intimate relationships was simple—derive the greatest amount of experience
without committing to the other person. I *would* commit
when I met my true partner, which I eventually did, but in the
absence of certainty or even probability, I permitted myself to
get involved because I was taken by a particular woman's
charms, because she didn't appear to require a commitment,
and because the involvement itself might have led to some
kind of commitment. This is a classic example of relationship
by default, which resonates with many men, and is in fact one
of "The Five Most Common Mistakes Men Make in Choosing a Partner," a talk I give as a professional relationship

counselor. I was involved in quite a few relationships by default in the twelve years I spent between marriages, most recently in the mid-eighties. These relationships were important to me because they were an opportunity to explore. They at first seemed innocuous to me, as it was relatively easy to withhold my emotions most of the time.

But I learned in my "no commitment" last relationship that I could not control how my partner felt, and that often I did not know how she felt or didn't want to know. When these uncommitted relationships ended, as they invariably did, their conclusions were often accompanied by a great deal of emotional turmoil and ugly recriminations, as my ex-partner would express considerable resentment at my having carried on a great deception, when again, all I wanted was someone to sleep with.

But it took the last relationship I had before I met my wife, Diane, to finally make me see that "no commitment" relationships didn't work for me, either. This was the mother of all nightmares breakups, the one whose ending was so painful that it truly changed my life. After this one, I swore off uncommitted relationships. I was like an alcoholic who goes on one binge too many and finally recognizes that he or she has no power to control the influence of strong drink. It was like that for me with relationships. After Claudia, I had to admit that I had no power over myself when it came to staying away from women who were not right for me, and I vowed that from that point on I would indulge only responsibly, that I would have to say to myself that I was consciously choosing to get involved with a particular person, rather than saying,

"Hey, what the heck, she seems interested and lovely, and nothing else is going on, so why not?"

Claudia and I had had a rocky time of it even when things were going smoothly. She and I were in different stages in life, even though we were roughly the same age. Although we liked each other, sort of, and even loved each other, in a manner of speaking, there was something about the two of us that prevented real domestic harmony, and every time we got on the subject of the future, a subject I tried to avoid at all costs, things turned ugly. I knew I wanted kids, that I was destined to be a father, that my childhood had been a positive experience and that I loved my own father very much. Being a parent was definitely in my game plan. She already had three teenage daughters and a hostile ex-husband, and her blueprint was to have no more children, which I could understand completely, and which acted as a solvent to our relationship whenever our ability to get along reasonably well for a month or two acted as a glue. I always knew that the day would come when we would no longer be together, despite her heroic but disingenuous assertions that she would consider having one child as a condition of our remaining as partners. I knew she wanted no more, that the ones she had brought her very little pleasure and a lot of grief. Besides, she struck me as someone who was not a particularly calm and sane mother, and would not turn into one even if she had a second chance. She was not the right partner for me, and it was just a matter of time before a permanent ending would be called for.

In fact, in the two plus years we spent together, we broke up six or seven different times, for periods ranging from one week to three months, and when we got back together in the fall of 1985, there was a part of me that knew it would be for the last time. My relationship-by-default mechanism was still very much in order, however, so I bravely signed on for another half-miserable / half-wonderful tour of duty with Claudia. When she surreptitiously read my journal nine months later and found out that I had been with another woman while she had been away on a business trip, she simply walked out of my apartment and my life. We never spoke to each other again, even though we lived in the same city, ran into each other on occasion, and had a very close mutual friend, Patricia, who by this time had moved back to New York.

It was the aftermath of the breakup that chilled me. Although she never confronted me directly, Claudia methodically tried to undermine my reputation as a "nice" person by telling everyone that I had had an affair while she was close to dying in Chicago on business. It is true that I had spent the night with someone else while she was gone, although in my mind I was already out of the relationship but did not have the courage to break it off, which I had tried to do numerous times before without success. But I knew that Claudia was insanely jealous, and although I did not deliberately put my journal on the coffee table for her to peruse, I was not unhappy that she found out about my infidelity because I knew this revelation would finally cause our relationship to be untenable for her.

It was also true that she was ill on her trip, and came home with pneumonia, but to say that I had an affair while she was on her deathbed was typical of the way she twisted and manipulated facts. In the final analysis, I was glad that we were through. My reputation, such as it was, would withstand her withering onslaught, and the sadness that we could never communicate in an adult way, which would have been healthier for both of us, stayed with me for a long time. I had dreams about her for years to come, and in one, which I related to my therapist, I noticed a tiny black speck on the fleshy part of my hand at the base of the thumb, and when I went to pull it out with my fingers, a huge black insect came out of my hand and unfolded itself. My therapist said that the dream indicated that I was in the process of resolving the pain of this relationship, and the insect represented all the things that did not work for me. The fact that it appeared to be a tiny speck and was really a big, black insect was an indication that much of what was unhealthy was beneath the surface, and the act of pulling it out was a very remedial one for me.

But the most positive upshot of this breakup was that it was so bad, and I knew I never wanted to experience another one. I resolved that relationship by default was no longer tolerable, and that I would not involve myself with anyone unless I could look at myself in the mirror and say that I could see myself being with this woman for at least ten years. If I couldn't, we would remain friends, no matter how much I desired her sexually or how much she desired me. The sixties and seventies had ended, at least for me.

One of the ways in which both men and women fool themselves is to stay in relationships that they know will not ultimately endure, with the understanding that they will meet someone else while they are still involved and thus will not have to face the breakup alone. That rarely works. Physical involvement implies emotional involvement, and holding on to a relationship that isn't right only prolongs the period during which no one who is right will appear. One may have affairs, but people with whom one has affairs are rarely people with whom one has enduring relationships, and so they aren't right either. Suddenly, freed from any involvement with Claudia, save for my solitary attempts to "process" the meaning of this sad involvement, I was faced with many possibilities that seemed worth exploring. I resolved to make having an intimate partner the number one priority in my life, and for me that meant being open to any and all possibilities. These included trying to resurrect a relationship with someone from my past, which wasn't right then and, it was clear, almost immediately, wasn't right now, and being available when one of my friends or acquaintances wanted to introduce me to someone. I always marvel when someone tells me that they've never been on a blind date before. I laugh and usually say that to me it's a necessary part of one's emotional education, like reading *Catcher in the Rye* or going to a baseball game.

I also have to laugh—actually to keep from crying—when I run across people who profess with all sincerity to be looking for their true partners, and will not go out with someone who lives more than thirty minutes away, as if they intend to spend their entire relationship in some perpetual state of dating limbo. Geographically undesirable, it's called. It makes me shake my head in sorrow and pity, for where one lives can change in an instant, and if one is truly serious about finding a mate, where that man or woman lives has no place on any list of qualities. Love has nothing to do with convenience.

In fact, during the twelve years I spent between marriages, I went to New York on one blind date and Los Angeles on another. Isn't that what airplanes are for, to bring together people who are tied by business, family, friendship, or possibly love? If someone I knew said I should meet someone they knew—and the result could be love—then I trusted my friend or acquaintance enough to say yes. Some would call this desperation. To them I say that the whole world is my backyard, that rigidity is to me the enemy, and that my intention to have love in my life ought to surpass all else.

So when I answered a personal ad placed by a woman who seemed very appealing to me, in *The New York Review of Books*, the fact that she lived in New York and I in California did not in any way dissuade me. In fact it only contributed to my excitement, to the romantic part of me. Of course it's always a long shot when you travel three thousand miles to meet someone, but it's a long shot when you walk three blocks to meet someone at a neighborhood café, and he or she lives three blocks in the other direction. At least we knew we enjoyed the same publication, and since I could plan our date around a few business meetings and visit friends as well, Jill and I set something up by telephone.

Although nine years had passed since I lived in the city, I had been back many times and enjoyed what it offered without having to put up with what I didn't like about it. The four- or five-day trips I took to New York are among my fondest memories, and I especially liked to be in the Big Apple in the fall, when the air is crisp and perfect for long walks up and down the avenues. My transcontinental conversations with Jill were a promising beginning, as we shared a lot of common interests, compatible political views, Jewish upbringings, and a desire to contribute to a better world. She was a public defender, and I was the executive director of a think tank that dealt with world hunger. On paper we were a good match, but that's like saying that an employer and prospective employee are a good match on the strength of a résumé alone. Nothing substitutes for actual time spent together. I made reservations at an Italian restaurant in the Village that had been recommended to me, called Cent' Anni (One Hundred Years), and arrived in town with both great expectations and a realistic notion that this would at best be a long shot. We had exchanged photos, but I have found in more than six years of matchmaking that the most important component in determining if attraction exists is not a person's looks but the compatibility of two individual energies—a concept even more mysterious than "chemistry" or "attractiveness," or any other of the vague bromides single people use to eliminate potential partners from consideration—and compatible energies must be tested in person.

This is not to say that chemistry cannot develop, which in fact it does, even between two people who are not mad about each other from the very beginning, but one must be willing to allow that possibility to occur, and in the case of two people living on opposite sides of the continent, there would have to be something pretty strong at the outset to justify keeping a flame going.

I was staying not far from the restaurant with my friends the Sweeneys, whom I had known and loved for twelve years, almost from the first time we talked. They lived in a converted loft in the Flatiron district, and I was a frequent guest of theirs after I had left the city. They were models to me in many ways, both as parents and as friends, and their generosity and goodwill when I was a struggling student is something I will never forget. On this occasion, they not only offered me their couch, as they had done on numerous occasions over the years, but their car as well. Jill lived in Brooklyn, and they insisted that I hold on to the option of driving her home at the end of the evening, that that would be the gentlemanly thing to do.

They also reminded me that this was New York, and that the sight of car radios was an open invitation for thieves and other undesirables to break in and steal them. Wherever I parked the car, they stressed, whether it was on the street or in a lot, I was to remove the radio and put it under the front seat. Under no circumstances was I to leave the radio in the dash. Pat Sweeney, who had been present when I had done dumb things before, made me repeat three times that I would not leave the radio in the dash. I did what he said and, he being a lapsed Catholic married to a Jew, crossed myself for his benefit.

I drove the short distance to the Village, found a spot on the street, removed the radio, placed it under the front seat, and walked into the restaurant. Jill and I introduced ourselves and I could immediately tell that in one respect we were not on the same wavelength. I had anticipated this rendezvous for some time, had traveled a great distance to be there, and could not help but attach romantic feelings to the date. This was the case whether I saw Jill again or not. I had donned a sharp suit, chosen an intimate spot, and had arrived with a flower. Jill, apparently, had entered into this little encounter with lower expectations. She wore plain boots, although it wasn't particularly cold outside, a drab sweater over a long hippie-type skirt, and immediately announced that she wouldn't be drinking any wine because of a bladder infection. She turned out not to be very hungry, and this long-awaited "romantic" dinner, to which I had looked forward for three weeks, was over in forty-five minutes. She ordered an appetizer, didn't want dessert, and somehow the absence of a bottle on the table made everything else move fast. Romance is abetted by lingering, but it was clear on some level—aside from her affliction, which was unfortunate—that she did not have the same degree of romantic sensibility as I, that she was more practical, that food and drink were for her more a biological necessity and less an expression of sensuality, and that the task of saving the world by helping indigent clients was more important than anything else. Again, she obviously wasn't at her best, and perhaps I would have wanted to see her again had we lived in the same city, but it was becoming increasingly clear that there wasn't enough between us to merit a transcontinental relationship. Finding a partner is like learning to walk. You fall down, you get up and try again. Deciding to give up your search after a bad date is like a one-year-old deciding not to walk after bumping his head. I watched my sons fall hundreds of times before they could consistently steady themselves, and never once did they show any hesitation about getting back up again. It's the same with romance. You learn from what happens and keep going. And when it finally does "click" with someone, it is all the sweeter because of all the dates with people that didn't work out.

Perhaps to salvage the evening, I offered to drive her home. Since it was only eight-thirty, and she wasn't feeling well, it seemed like the right thing to do. She accepted, and seemed to perk up in the car. Maybe she just didn't like restaurants, but that would have been a problem because I love them. Anyway, she talked about her life, her work, her friends and family, and I mostly listened and chimed in when appropriate. I was beginning to form a second opinion about her. She was obviously bright, sensitive, and articulate. We were really starting to connect when she mentioned she had a friend who lived on President Street in Park Slope, which reminded me that my friend Patricia, who was friends with Claudia, and who had just moved to Brooklyn, lived on President Street. I suggested that we prolong the evening by trying to find her. I didn't know her address and didn't have her number, but maybe it was the lawyer in Jill, the investigator, that responded. She loved the idea. First we tried by phone, and then possible addresses came to mind, and after a few dead ends that could easily have daunted us, we actually rang Patricia's doorbell, and she answered, taken aback to say the least and unsure of what to make of my arrival with a strange woman.

But Patricia also knew my adventurous side, and had in fact fixed me up on another blind date in New York when we both lived in San Francisco in the early eighties, and so she wasn't surprised to hear that I had come to New York for the same reason. Patricia had also always been a reality check for me, and although she liked Claudia, she never thought we were right for each other. There was a part of me that wanted her to meet Jill, and the two of them hit it off instantly. We talked and had tea and then decided to get a bite nearby. Patricia's brother, who was visiting from Florida, joined us and we had a quick snack at a noisy restaurant. Jill's appetite had improved, and she had really become enlivened during the hour we had spent at Patricia's place, and so when we walked back to the car, parked across from Patricia's apartment, shortly after midnight, things seemed promising. The evening was even beginning to feel romantic. I was free the next night, and Jill had already hinted at getting together again. One thing was for certain—we wouldn't be going to Cent' Anni.

As we said good-bye to Patricia and her brother, I could feel my stomach turn and my throat tighten as I suddenly saw that I had forgotten to heed Patrick's advice about putting the radio under the seat. The car had been broken into, and wires stuck out where the radio had been. Shattered glass was everywhere. It was Zimmerman's garage door all over again. When we had parked on President Street an hour and a half before and rang Patricia's doorbell, it was if I had never heard Patrick's instructions. That's how far in the deep recesses of my memory they had vanished. I was completely consumed with the hunt for Patricia's apartment and with trying to decide whether I was enjoying Jill enough to want to see her again. I was reminded of my own dictum about New York—

that you could love it but it will never love you. It had lashed out at me again. It can be such an unforgiving place.

We went back into Patricia's apartment to call the police, and I realized that I had not felt so bad in quite some time. I had been warned and had forgotten, this long-anticipated romantic evening had turned out to be nothing if not a ride on a roller-coaster, my friend's car window was smashed and his radio gone, it was now almost one o'clock in the morning and I was on the phone with the local police, and all my past mistakes and disappointments were flashing through my mind. But all of this did not even compare to the horror I felt when I noticed something on the bulletin board in Patricia's kitchen while I was on hold with the precinct.

It was a quote, not from Socrates, or Spinoza, or Oscar Wilde, or Madame Curie, and not something meant to inspire when all seems lost. The quote was from, of all people, Claudia, and it was so typical of her that I could not imagine this sentiment having been expressed by anyone else. It had been four months since our last encounter and the wound in me had not healed. So when I saw the words "Just a dick connected to another fucked-up man—Claudia," I immediately concluded that it referred to me, and that somehow Patricia either agreed with her in principle or God-forbid in the particular. At that moment in my life, I felt so low, so diminished, so ugly and unworthy. It was all I could do to remember why I was standing in my friend's kitchen. I wanted nothing but to screw myself down into the floor and disappear forever. I felt terrible, my mouth was dry, my stomach was tied up in knots, and I knew I would have to face the Sweeneys in the morning and tell them what had happened.

I couldn't confront Patricia at that moment. I was dealing with a broken window, a missing radio, my own feelings of guilt and inadequacy, and I was three thousand miles from home. The fact that I was on a blind date during all this had become almost insignificant to me. All I wanted to do was take Jill home and be alone. When I dropped her off she compassionately asked if I wanted to come up for a cup of tea but I politely declined and said I would call her later in the day to see about going out again that night. Of course everything depended on what Sweeney and I would have to do with the car, so it was hard for me to make any kind of commitment.

The ride back to Manhattan was frigid, the air blowing through the car a constant reminder of my faux pas. I told the Sweeneys at breakfast what had happened and it was hard for them not to be angry with me, even though they were trying to be understanding at the same time. They reminded me that I had promised to remove the radio, but what could I say? I felt like a child who is learning to go to the potty and has an accident. I fucked up. There was no getting around it. It's amazing how we allow for children to make mistakes or not know how to do something right, but when it comes to adults, *especially with ourselves,* we tend to be less forgiving, at least right away. I wanted to help Pat deal with replacing the window, and we took off to try to fix it. He wanted to get it done off the books, so we drove deep into the South Bronx, where they deal in busted auto glass.

It was not a joyful experience. We drove there in the morning, talked to someone with a heavy Spanish accent, and were told to hang on. The fact that there were perhaps ten or fifteen other people in the same predicament was not very encouraging. We waited and waited in the deepening cold for hours, and every time we asked Popeye, which was the name of the guy we had spoken to, if we were next, he would only say "Soon," or "After that guy," or "I'm getting it." Finally he came over, after we had been there for four hours, and said he didn't have the glass. He suggested we drive to another place on Jerome Avenue and we did, but they were closed. It was by this time late afternoon and the glass still had not been replaced, and since it was Saturday, there was little likelihood that it would. Pat was by this time calm about what had happened—I could tell by the fact that he was teasing me again—and I offered to write him a check to cover everything, since I was leaving the next day.

I called Jill to tell her that I was exhausted and emotionally wrung out after spending an unsuccessful day in the South Bronx. She was sympathetic to my mood. I didn't know how to leave things with her, since I was returning home, so I didn't say anything, but somehow I knew that it was unlikely that I would see her again. It is possible that things would have worked out differently had our meeting not ended as it did, but I'll never know. Perhaps if we had gone out again that night the entire course of my life would have changed, but maybe this was the universe's way of saying that we weren't true partners, and that I was not destined to enter into another relationship by default, especially a transcontinental one. In fact, we never did see each other again.

Pat fixed the window and got another radio, and I stopped feeling awful about what had happened. Learning to forgive is tough enough, but learning to forgive oneself is probably the most difficult thing in life to learn. Cars are reparable and replaceable, and I have learned over the years, especially since my life was blessed with children, that there are things in life that are important and other things that are not, and cars fall into the second category. What was important was that my friendship with the Sweeneys survived.

Later I confronted Patricia about the quote. She said it didn't refer to me but I suspected she was just trying to spare my feelings. At that point it didn't matter, because there was something about seeing those words that liberated me from any lingering bad feelings about the ending of my relationship with Claudia. It was almost like an inoculation. I got over it and the sting didn't hurt anymore.

I went out on more blind dates—this time closer to home—and so my transcontinental rendezvous with Jill turned out to be the last of its kind. I realized that I enjoy life's luxuries, that practicality isn't enough for me, and when I met Diane ten weeks later and saw that she also had a nice blend of both, I knew there was great potential. The fact that we were engaged six weeks after we met only confirmed the obvious, that we were and still are meant to be for each other.

But I also firmly believe that meeting her was made

possible by, even built on, everything that preceded it, from my first marriage, to Judy, to my relationship with Betsy, and even with Claudia. Without all this, no relationship with Diane would have been possible. For Diane fell in love with the person she encountered, and that person was the sum total of all that had come before—what worked and what didn't, the risks that paid off and the ones that didn't—and so regardless of what happens to me, I always see my experience as uniquely mine, that which defines me in contrast to everyone else. I try not to judge what happens on its face value, for it is only in time that one can understand real significance, freed from the emotions that invariably take over in the midst of a dramatic event or occurrence. Yes, that night was an ugly, upsetting one. But it was also kind of romantic in its own way, the way my feelings for Jill went through a number of permutations before the reality of New York set in to wipe them out entirely. And seeing the quote truly helped me to purge the last vestiges of Claudia from my consciousness. I was now free to love another, and it is no surprise to me that it wasn't long after that I did. That night was a capsule summary of life—bittersweet.

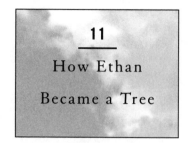

11

How Ethan

Became a Tree

ONE DAY I was playing in the backyard of our home in California with my son Julian, who was five years old at the time, when the ball with which we were playing rolled to a stop under a medium-sized flowering plum tree, which we call Ethan's Tree, a splotch of deep dark red in the mostly green yard.

As I bent to pick up the ball, I heard Julian asking me a question in his most earnest voice.

"Daddy, how did Ethan become a tree?"

"Well, it's a long, long story," I replied.

"I was always wondering about that, why Ethan is a tree."

"Do you know who Ethan is?" I asked.

"No."

"Do you mind if I tell the story using grown-up words?"

"No, but I hope I can understand it," he replied.

"I think you will. You might not know every word, but I think you'll be able to follow. I'll start at the beginning."

There was a commercial once for Remington Electric shavers, in which Victor Kiam said that he loved the Remington Electric shaver so much he bought the company. In my case, I went to a matchmaking service upon the recommendation of a friend, who said that she had heard from a friend of hers that the matchmaker had a lot of integrity. Well, I liked the matchmaker so much I married her.

One of the many things I liked about Diane was that she wanted to have children as much as I did, and after the Claudia debacle this was a welcome relief. When we got married, seven months after we met, we managed to arrange a rather long honeymoon, which was made possible by a series of fortunate developments and a sense of adventure that we realized we shared the first time we went out. We were away in Italy and much of Europe for four months, and soon after we returned to the United States in early December, we found out that Diane was pregnant with our first child.

He or she had been conceived in a small but charming hotel room on the Boulevard Saint-Michel in Paris, to which we had traveled after leaving a farmhouse in Italy, which had been our base. Both Diane and I were ecstatic to find out that she was going to have a baby so soon, as were our parents. My in-laws already had four grandchildren at that point, but for my parents this child would be their first, and there was something about what my mother endured during World War II that made this event a very special one. Diane chose a doctor who would handle the delivery, a kind and gentle man who was supported by a team of midwives, and the hospital was not far from our apartment in San Francisco, into which I had moved shortly after she and I were engaged.

As the first weeks passed into months, and as Diane's belly swelled with the incremental growth of our first baby, our sense of awe at the very miracle of life grew along with a recognition of how blessed we were. We had met barely a year before, fallen in love almost immediately, were engaged six weeks later, married six months after that, left our respective jobs to spend four months in Europe, and had returned home not quite a year later to find out that we were pregnant. It was difficult in some ways to take in all this good fortune. The year had been filled with such excitement that I felt I had grabbed the tail of a tiger and was on a ride that I could barely control.

And now I was staring fatherhood directly in the face. I was working with Diane's family in various capacities, so I was also the proverbial son-in-law who gets taken into the family business. If we had lived on the East Coast, this story might have become a cliché, but there was something about all this taking place in California that saved it, at least in my mind, from being just another Jewish story.

Diane was the model of health. She didn't smoke, barely drank an ounce of alcohol or caffeine, and her diet consisted of wholesome, nutritious food. She participated in a yoga class for pregnant women, and one day, while she was lying on the couch reading a magazine, she looked up and said that she loved her life, that she had never been happier at any time, and she couldn't imagine anything better than the present moment. Here she was, in our small but lovely apartment, with a view of a great city like San Francisco through the window, together with the man she loved, pregnant, with such vivid memories of married life that already included adventure and world travel, and feeling wonderful. Our baby was due on August 8—8/8/88—and although we knew the chance was slim that he or she would arrive when expected, still Diane, who places great stock in numbers, thought that the due date was a sign that this child would be special.

"So the baby was growing in Mommy's tummy," said Julian, with an air of resolute certainty.

"That's right. Do you know how it got there?"

"No," he replied. "Well, is it because you love Mommy?"

"Yes, sort of. I'll explain it better some day, sweetie, but right now I want to continue with the story."

"OK."

"Do you like this story?"

He shrugged. "It's all right. It's kind of long."

"Well, I want to make sure I don't leave out anything important."

"OK."

By May it was clear we had certain matters to decide. The baby was due in less than three months and we were living in a one-bedroom apartment three flights up, not the best arrangement with a newborn. We started to look for a house to rent in Marin County, across the Golden Gate Bridge just north of the city, a beautiful area with a string of small towns, and a reputation as one of California's touchy-feely places. I had never lived there, but Diane had, years before. I had a lot of hesitation about moving out of San Francisco. I love cities

and had always lived in them as an adult. Since I left Philadelphia more than twenty-five years ago I had not returned to
the suburbs, and it was hard to imagine leaving San Francisco,
where I had prospered and developed roots. But Diane was
persuading me. If I had liked the countryside near Rome—
and I had, *molto*—then I would like Marin. Although it was
suburban, in the sense of being near a major American city,
there were neighborhoods that didn't have houses that all
looked the same, like the one in which I had grown up. Give it
a chance, she kept saying, we can always come back to the city
if we don't like it.

I relented. Within days we were tromping through the
picture-perfect towns of Marin—Mill Valley, Larkspur, San
Anselmo, San Rafael, Fairfax, Sausalito—to try to find the
place in which our little addition would be born and spend the
first year of his or her life. We had an idea of what we wanted
to pay, which was considerably higher than what we were
paying where we lived, but we thought we could manage the
increase. After all, a baby needs a room of its own, and it was
becoming increasingly difficult for Diane to trudge up and
down the stairs every day.

By this time the baby had a name—Baci, Italian for
kisses—and a presence. She or he was easy to see, because
Diane's stomach would move when the baby extended an arm
or leg, and she often let my hand rest on her stomach to feel
the kicks that indicated that Baci was fine. Diane's regular
visits to the doctor and midwives were indicating a normal
pregnancy with no complications. She was now in her seventh
month with a little more than two to go when we found a

house to rent on a quiet, beautiful street in the flat part of Mill Valley. It was a lovely three-bedroom place with a family room and beautiful landscaped grounds on three sides. The landlady liked us immediately, and we were ready to sign a lease. We would move in July 1, a little more than a month before Baci was due, and it would give us enough time to fix up the house, get the right equipment, although not too much, as there is a superstition in Judaism about getting baby stuff before the baby, and prepare for our new life as parents.

By this time we were also in a birthing class at the hospital in San Francisco where Diane was going to deliver. There were fourteen couples who came each week and I remember sitting there during the third or fourth class and thinking that something unexpected could happen to any one of us. Here are all these happy mothers and fathers to be, each eagerly anticipating the arrival of a person who will change their lives, and at any time something unforeseen, unexpected, unwelcome could occur. I quickly dismissed these fears as just that—fears—and I looked around the room at everyone and hoped that God would keep all of us and our babies safe. I left this disturbing but vivid line of thinking, and returned to the present, which happened to be massaging Diane's neck and shoulders while she sat peacefully in front of me.

Memorial Day weekend was upon us, and we had much to take care of with the house, in addition to a party that was scheduled for Monday. On Saturday as we were getting dressed in the morning to drive across the bridge to Mill Valley to sign the lease, Diane called me over to feel the baby kicking. I put my hand on her stomach as I had done hundreds of times before and felt a series of strong movements that seemed more vigorous than other kicks I had felt, and I remarked that he or she was really getting a good workout today.

We completed our business and spent the next five days in a kind of reverie. I had never been happier. I was about to be a father, I had a bright future, a lovely wife, great friends, and now I was going to be living in a beautiful little house, which I fell in love with the first time I saw it, on a tranquil street about twenty-five minutes from San Francisco. There was now going to be plenty of room to spread out, no stairs to have to climb, and a baby to care for. At age thirty-nine, I was finally going to be a father, something I had always longed for but had wondered when I would have the opportunity to experience.

On Monday night we had returned from the party, which was an outdoor affair in which we both ate a lot of perfectly done barbecued oysters. Diane came out of the bath and said that she couldn't remember the last time she had felt the baby. It wasn't as if she remembered not feeling the baby, it was just that with all the excitement of the past few days, she wasn't aware of him or her, and now, when she put her hand on her stomach, she couldn't feel him kicking. This was not a cause for alarm in and of itself, because babies of course do sleep in the womb and aren't always going to kick on demand, but the fact that she couldn't remember the last time she felt him concerned her, and in my mind I could only go back to Saturday morning, when I had felt about twenty rapid kicks.

We tried for hours to detect the signs that we had grown

used to feeling—movement, kicks, heartbeat—but we were unable to get any kind of response. Diane drank some juice, as the sugar is supposed to stimulate the baby to move around, but this also did not produce any discernible signs. At one point I thought I had detected a heartbeat, but I wasn't sure, and even this signal was a weak and tenuous substitute for the certainty that the baby was alive and kicking, which had been our reality just a few days before. Diane said she would call the doctor in the morning.

In the hours between the time she said she hadn't re-membered feeling the baby and the time we fell asleep, we never once discussed the possibility that something had gone wrong. It was as if our life together up to that point had been so fairy-tale–like that it was inconceivable that anything could have happened to our child. We knew the risk of miscarriage, that many pregnancies spontaneously end in the first trimester from a variety of causes, and we were cautious in our enthusi-asm during that time as a result of this information. But once that point passed, we just assumed that everything would work out fine, and that the baby would be born healthy and full term on or about 8/8/88. And now, on 6/1/88, we found ourselves walking the few short blocks to Mount Zion Hospital to see what the ultrasound would turn up. We were in denial.

It seemed to take forever for the pediatric nurse to squeeze the goop on the piece that moves along the stomach of the mother, but as soon as she turned on the machine, I wished she hadn't. I looked at her and could tell immediately that she was undergoing a battle royal between her emotions and her professional demeanor, because she was going to be the one to have to tell us that our baby was dead. She continued to run that piece around and around to try to detect movement or hear a heartbeat, but the look of stone sadness on her face never changed. Diane was by this time sobbing as she clutched my hand, and at one point I definitely heard a heartbeat and—barely able to speak—inquired about it. The nurse just shook her head and said in an equally inaudible voice that it was the mother's. At that point, we had just within moments found out that the term no longer applied to Diane.

"Why did the baby die?" asked Julian, obviously affected by the story.

"We didn't know."

"Did you ever find out?"

"Not really," I said. "Different people had different ideas about what happened, but no one really knows for sure."

"Was his name Ethan?"

"Yes."

"Is he in the tree?"

"I don't know. I think so. I think he's everywhere."

There are moments in the life of anyone who has ever lived when he or she knows that what is happening is one of the worst things to have ever happened, and in my and Diane's case, nothing had ever come close. There had never been any tragedies, any serious illnesses. Our parents were alive, we had not lost any siblings, not experienced any personal harm or sustained terror, and it had never entered our minds that our baby would be a special human being in this particular way, that it would die before it was born.

We were in a state of shock, incapable of believing that so

close to the end of this pregnancy something as heartbreaking as a stillbirth would happen to us. As word spread through the day among our families and friends, the reality set in. Our life was not the same as it had been just a few days before. We were experiencing for the first time sudden loss, the stark truth that there was nothing we could do to bring our baby back, that we would have to accept this development as surely as we accept the fact that day follows night. For now, locked as we were in our numbing, all-encompassing grief, Diane would have to go through the process of giving birth. The medical team thought it best to induce labor, not to wait for a "spontaneous evacuation" that might or might not happen. Already that night, as we were preparing to go to bed before having to be back in the hospital at nine the next morning, I could see that Diane's stomach had shrunk, not considerably but in a way that a balloon that is slowly losing its air gets smaller. The process inside had already begun.

Intense periods of weeping can bring about a certain sense of physical relief that actually soothes our grieving—for a time. And yet we knew it was impossible to fully experience the depth of our loss because of what was in store the next morning. No one could predict how long this labor would take or what the doctors would find, if anything, about the baby. While Diane quietly sobbed herself to sleep, I read, for the first time in my life voluntarily, because it seemed to me a good idea, the Twenty-third Psalm. I had had to memorize it in the fifth grade, and it was at this tender, grief-stricken moment, nearly thirty years later, when what I needed above all was consolation, that the full import of what was contained in King David's poem of acceptance, surrender, and faith struck me: "The Lord is my shepherd, I shall not want . . . He restoreth my soul . . . Yea, though I walk through the valley of the shadow of death, I will fear no evil, for Thou art with me, Thy rod and Thy staff, they comfort me . . . My cup runneth over. . . ."

It was the first time I had ever turned to the Bible—Old Testament or New—for solace, and it worked. I had always relied on logic, on reason, to figure out problems. But at this point in my life, using logic and reason was tantamount to eating weak, watery soup when one is ravenously hungry. I needed something to sink my teeth into and I found it in the Twenty-third Psalm: "Surely, goodness and mercy shall follow me all the days of my life, and I will dwell in the House of the Lord forever." Weeping, I put down the poetry of David the King and heard Diane's soft, rhythmic breathing. I suddenly felt stronger, capable of dealing with my life. And although I wasn't the one who was going to have to go through the procedure in the morning, I knew that Diane would deal with her life as well.

I slept peacefully and when I awoke, there was a moment of incomprehension before becoming fully aware, when for an instant I did not realize that I was no longer about to be a father. My first impulse was to recall the heartbreaking news that I had learned the previous day, but my second was to assure myself that it was only a dream, that I had opened my eyes to the certainty that Diane was still pregnant, and that we would be having a healthy, active baby in a couple of months. But then the cold, stark reality of what had actually happened took over, and the totality of my being—past, present, and future—was called upon to contribute to an emotional strength that I had never heretofore had to display. I gently shook Diane, and we held each other a long time, crying and saying we loved each other, and within an hour or two she was lying on a hospital bed. The medical team had already begun to induce labor.

We could not have foreseen such an ordeal. All through the day, Diane was poked, prodded, drugged with one type of substance or another, and still that baby would not come out. I succeeded in holding my emotions pretty much in check, until I was walking down the corridor outside Diane's room and saw on the patient board next to her name the large letters "FD," for fetal demise, and it was only then that the full magnitude of what had just taken place hit me, that unlike every other woman in the maternity ward of Mount Zion Hospital on June 2, 1988, my wife, Diane, was trying to give birth to a dead baby, going through all the struggles, the pains, the exhaustion, the macabre moments of humor, all the agony of childbirth, to expel from her body a boy or girl who would never cry, never spill its food, never bump its head on a kitchen cabinet or write with colored markers on a hotel room wall, and never look at me at bedtime when I asked what the best part of the day was and say, "Now." I erupted in long, uncontrollable sobs, and I didn't care who heard me. A hospital counselor was very understanding and said that I didn't have to censor myself.

It was also that day that I learned what real intimacy is between two people who are committed to each other. I saw

Diane in a way that no one had ever seen her—barely in control of herself, dazed, disheveled, overcome with grief, without any modesty regarding body parts or body functions that had to be carried out in front of all present, and it occurs to me now that people who dream of a relationship and do not think about what follows the romantic stage don't really know what true intimacy is, when their partner is vulnerable in a way that might have been inconceivable just moments before. Not only was I a man in the delivery room, I was also dealing with death and grief, being supportive of my partner, and also trying to make rational decisions about what to do medically.

Finally, very late in the day, the first signs that all the interventions had begun to take effect occurred, and shortly after midnight on June 3, 1988, our first child, a boy, was born fully formed and without life. We wrapped him in a blanket and held him, and said what a beautiful little boy he was. We took his picture with a Polaroid camera, made a footprint of both feet, and called him Ethan, a name we had considered during the pregnancy and that seemed appropriate for him, since he was already part of the ether.

We left the hospital later in the morning. This was a particularly hard time for Diane, who cried on the way out because of her empty arms and full breasts. I looked at her flat stomach and could not believe what I saw. This woman, who had gained twenty-seven pounds during the previous seven and a half months, now looked to me like it had all been a dream. The sun was shining, the air was warm, and the first thing I said to Diane was that I didn't care what happened, I still wanted to move into the house we had found. Diane agreed with me immediately. I was not going to let this loss prevent me from living. Although a major life dream had died, there would be other dreams, and somehow I knew that going ahead with our plans was the right thing to do.

Although there was no infant to take advantage of the bounty, Diane's milk came in and she had to bind her breasts to try to slow down the flow. It was such a strange time. Friends came by to grieve with us, and talking about the baby and the experience made us both feel better. We laughed, we cried, we talked about how incredible it was to hold our baby, and we said that we were just as committed to the idea of being parents and even more committed to each other than ever before.

Diane stayed home for a few days. I couldn't even think about work and hung around with her for a week or so. The strangest moments for me were when I would go out to buy groceries or take care of some detail or another, and would notice little children playing on the street or in a park. Sometimes my heart would fill up with joy to see that these little creatures actually did exist, and I would smile and look at them with wonder and amusement. At other times I would break into tears at the sight of a toddler holding her mother's hand. The scene would be too excruciating to look at, and I never knew what reaction I would have. It was completely unpredictable. And yet both responses soothed me. It was as if deep in my body there was a wisdom that knew precisely how to react in a given moment. Mixed together in a tangle of emotion were love for Diane, grief at having lost a child I never got to hear, and a sense of having been elevated from ordinary, daily life into something quite extraordinary. I also had the feeling that I had been again touched—literally touched—by death, and that it had taken my son, or rather that he had chosen it over life at this point, and it consoled me to reflect on death as something of an unwanted guest in our culture, a presence that lurks in the shadows but is hardly ever invited to participate. Yet it is the final truth of everyone's life, at least the life we know.

The circumstances of Ethan's short life and sudden death were also strange to me. How does one grieve for someone he has never really known, but who has been such a central figure in one's life? It's even more difficult to mourn with friends and relatives who didn't know him at all, who only knew that Diane was pregnant and were excited for us. And yet through all this I came to develop a grudging respect for death, for the final act of life, for the fact that no one ever knows how the last chapter of his or her life will be written, and in this case, the end came very soon for a child who had yet to be born. But death was now a fact of my little boy's life, and that was reason enough for me to have different feelings about it. It somehow no longer seemed so dreadful, so foreign, so final. It had come into my life in a very intimate way and I decided to welcome it, to enter into a relationship with it, not to turn it away or deny its presence. It was now not only a reality for Pop Pop Peter, who had gone to meet it for me, and for Bubby, who had also died in the intervening years, but now it held my first child in its grip, and I had no way of knowing what that meant. There was thus no reason to think that it wasn't a benign thing, like puberty, adulthood, the advance of old age, or any other passage in life.

There was also something else I began to notice about a week after Ethan was born, after the pain and shock of the event had begun to wear off. I felt as if life had become hyper-vivid, as if everything were suddenly crystal clear to me, that each situation carried with it an embedded guide that explained exactly what was going on. There was suddenly no need to calculate, to evaluate, to judge. I recognized that there was a place within me that knew everything I needed to know, that did not need to weigh, that could see right through the thin veneer of superficial social life to the core of reality. Suddenly I knew the "truth" of living, and to me that meant following my dreams, whatever they were, regardless of whether they were momentary, like pausing to look at an interesting window display, or holding on to a dream like being a writer and living in Italy. The one thing I realized above all in the enlightened state, which didn't last very long and in fact ended as soon as I returned to the exigencies of the "real" world, was that one never knows how long any one particular lifetime will last, and that waiting for some other time to pursue one's dreams might mean that they never happen. There is no other time. There is only now.

Diane and I also saw that if we wanted to have a family we were really going to have to be courageous and affirm that that was what we really wanted, because it would have been easy at that point to hold back and put off trying to climb that particular peak again. We had gotten so close to the summit, only to fall back in disillusionment and sorrow. But in that hyper-real state, in a state of grace really, it seemed remarkably easy to hold on to our faith in ourselves, in our abilities, our dreams, and even our goodness. Ethan taught us a valuable lesson, one that is heard often but rarely experienced. The lesson is that the material body is but one aspect of reality, of life, of living, and that a person can live on even if he or she was here for a blink of an eye and no one knew him or her. Ethan came into our lives for less than nine months and irrevocably changed them, for his presence gave us both a kind of courage we lacked before—the courage to live, to live fully and deeply, to not be dependent on the opinions of others, to follow pathways that seem to promise to take us to where we want to go, and, finally, never to be afraid. If we could endure the loss of our child, we could endure much more than we ever thought.

We cremated him and invited everyone with whom we were close to a memorial service at our new home in Mill Valley on the day he was to have been born. Our families and friends were in attendance. Diane's doctor and midwife were there and spoke about our ordeal, and it was a touching and cathartic moment for everyone who really hadn't known what to say to us to help us deal with our loss. But the main event of the afternoon was the planting of a young flowering plum tree sapling that would always remind us of Ethan, and that came to be called Ethan's Tree.

"But we don't live there anymore," said Julian, who was a bit confused.

"That's right, we lived there only a year before we moved into this house."

"Where was I?"

"Well, we didn't know it at the time, but when we

planted Ethan's Tree you were already growing in Mommy's tummy."

"When did I come out?"

"The next spring. And then two months later we moved into this house."

"But if you planted Ethan's Tree at the other house, how come it's here now?"

"Because we moved it. We didn't want to leave Ethan behind."

Just then, our other son, Elliott, who was two years old at the time, toddled into the backyard, refreshed from his nap and ready to play ball with us. I looked at these two healthy, beautiful, vibrant boys, my sons, and I looked again at Ethan's Tree, and as devastating as the loss of Ethan was for Diane and me, I can't deny that I now have what I wanted all along—to be a father and have the opportunity to live moments like the very one I was living, telling my sons how Ethan became a tree. And I also knew that had Ethan lived we wouldn't have had Julian, who was conceived six weeks after he died, and we wouldn't have had Elliott, since we probably would have stopped after two kids, as we have now, and it is inconceivable to me now to see life without these two bambini, that I would not trade the experience of being their father for all the tea in China, and that they would not have been a part of my life had Ethan not chosen to pass on to some other realm that I will know much more about when I get there myself.

And so things work out the way they do, not always the way we intend, and although we have free will and it is our birthright to exercise it, we still have to realize that the powers of life and death are far beyond our grasp, and that to live as if any moment could be our last, as if life were some kind of gift that was given to us by a donor of whom we know very little, and will be taken back from us at a time and a place that we have only so much influence over, is probably the most profound idea we can think. And this anonymous donor, who encompasses everything that ever was and ever will be, whose intelligence is of such a magnitude that it makes our use of the term laughable, is called by some people God. But it doesn't really matter what you call it, only that you live in a way that honors the gift.

"Daddy."

"Yes, Julian."

"Can we play baseball again?"

"Sure."

"Elliott's on your team. He's the fielder, you're the pitcher, and I'm the batter."

"What about Ethan? Can he play?" I inquired.

Julian paused for a moment, thinking about my question, wondering what I meant, whether to take it seriously. But then I could see that he had come up with a workable solution.

"Ethan can be the umpire," he replied.

Diane and I were acutely aware of how the people in our lives dealt with us immediately after Ethan died. Some of their behavior made us feel very uncomfortable, some of it was extremely soothing. We had a few conversations with people who called and then avoided the subject completely, as if it hadn't taken place. Others kept reassuring us that we would have other children, which turned out to be the case but which wasn't much comfort to us at the time. We didn't then want "other children." We wanted Ethan, and it was his loss that hurt us. Still others kept urging us to "get on" with our lives, whatever that meant, as if we had other options. I always thought that was a self-protective way of dealing with someone who has experienced a loss. If that person "gets on" with his or her life, then the one who is trying to be supportive presumably doesn't have to deal any longer with a grieving friend or relative.

But then other people we knew were wonderful. They came over and were really with us, comfortable being where we were, accepting of the fact that Diane and I were feeling tender and melancholy and dazed and resilient all at the same time. These people had no agenda other than to be present. If we wanted to talk about our ordeal, they were willing to listen. If we wanted to hear about what was going on with them, they were willing to talk. They had no apparent fear of us. If in the middle of a sentence Diane or I would break into tears, they didn't become uncomfortable and want to leave. And if for some reason I felt like being silly, hearing jokes or clowning around, that was fine too.

We also joined a support group for parents with neonatal loss, as it was called, and that helped as well. It was certainly ironic that in the same hospital building our old pregnancy group was still meeting while we were now on another wavelength, but it was oddly comforting to be with people who had had to endure similar experiences. We could talk openly about how we were getting on in the "real" world, and cry whenever we wanted without the fear of making someone uncomfortable. One couple's daughter had passed on four months after her birth, and I could not imagine how they could have endured losing a baby who had become part of their lives, but I realized by their response that a person's *attitude* toward what happens in life is infinitely more crucial than what happens when they said that they would not have traded the four months they spent with their daughter for anything, that they felt fortunate to have had that time together.

A couple we became friendly with for a time went on to have two healthy sons, as we did. And another woman, who knew that her stillborn baby probably represented the last time she could get pregnant and carry a child to term, went on to adopt several children, and seemed very happy with them when we saw her again recently. Time is a great healer, and does its work at its own pace. At the very moment of loss it is almost impossible to think of gain, but the latter never leaves us permanently.

In the profoundest sense, death is life's great equalizer. Whatever transpires in life, whatever differences exist between people on the material plane—whether in wealth or status, good fortune, or achievement—every single one of us is destined for the same next step. I do not use the word "end" to describe death, because I have no way of knowing that that is in fact the case, that death is an ending. Of course I recognize that it is an ending to this particular life but it very well may be the beginning of a new one or of something unimagined. Perhaps death is personal, and one experiences it and what lies beyond individually, according to one's image of it, just like the rest of life. This is how I see it, that death is whatever I want it to be, and for me, that means a true transcendence, a merging with all of creation. I cannot describe it more specifically than that, but I do know that the next phase of existence is a gain as well as a loss. Somehow Ethan taught me that.

12

Independence
Day

THE FOURTH OF July is not only the day on which the country celebrates its independence—the day also has special significance for me and my family. On that day, in 1990, I achieved another kind of independence, one that I had at certain times longed for, at other times struggled for, since I was old enough to recognize that I had a particular problem.

The loss of Ethan had had major reverberations for both Diane and me. Although she became pregnant and successfully delivered a healthy boy less than a year after his death, the psychological effects of losing him lingered. For me, the experience only confirmed what I had long believed—that life was a grand adventure, and that one should live to fulfill one's dreams, rather than endlessly putting them off into a future that usually never arrives. The ancient Romans had a phrase for this—carpe diem, seize the day.

My problem centered on work. This was unfortunate,

since one's work, along with whom one loves, and where one lives, are the three most fundamental aspects of living. For reasons that still baffle me, I had a difficult time figuring out how to apply carpe diem to career—knowing just what to do to make the many hours I spent working both remunerative and fulfilling at the same time. It seemed that my work was always one or the other.

I, like nearly everyone else, need money to live. I have had jobs that paid me handsomely, but which offered little in the way of another kind of nourishment—the kind that nourishes the soul, that makes one feel that one is exactly where one ought to be. With this kind of work, it is possible to wake up in the morning and look forward to performing the tasks of the day, so much so that the line between work and play becomes almost invisible.

This dilemma became more serious as the advent of marriage and family made my material requirements that much greater. When I was single, it was possible to monitor my material needs and live pretty much the way I wanted, but as soon as Diane and then Julian entered the picture, those decisions were no longer mine alone.

Ethan's death changed the equation. Before him, I could justify a career that really did nothing to nourish me emotionally but took care of my material needs, as long as I held on to the notion that one day I would do what truly satisfied me. At times, I had tried to follow a long-standing dream to make my living as a writer. I wrote two novels and a variety of short stories, but I had not managed to get them published, and had always fallen back on a "straight" job. My vow to keep up with my writing despite the fact that I was working "9 to 5" was usually just that—a vow—and was no more effective than an oft-repeated New Year's resolution to lose five pounds or be more patient with the kids. I did keep up with my personal journal, which I began more than twenty years ago and which has been a constant companion ever since.

So, although I was ostensibly the same person, with the same history and aspirations, the brief but moving appearance of Ethan in my life was like a bolt of lightning that illuminates what had previously been hidden in darkness. I could no longer wait for "tomorrow" to fulfill my dreams. I had to focus on what they really were, and live them. Ethan demonstrated to me that life was just as fleeting and unpredictable as all the philosophy books I had read had indicated. But the problem still remained. How could I shed my dependence on the corporate world when I earned significant money from it and had no idea how I could earn as much to support myself and my family without it?

I thought about my dilemma constantly, which I believe is the most effective first step in the realization of any dream. Although I was working with Diane's family in an executive capacity, it wasn't the right thing for me, and six months after Ethan died, four months before Diane was due to give birth to another baby, I decided to quit. I told Diane's dad that I would much rather have him as my father-in-law than my boss, and that I was leaving to pursue other means of supporting my family. He wished me well, and not for the first time in my life, but for the first time since I was married to Diane, I was unemployed.

Diane was completely supportive of my decision. She is ardently committed to the idea of living one's dreams, and at that point in time, a little more than a year after we were married, we had many of them. After having started an introduction service for another organization, which was the vehicle for our encounter, she wanted to start her own. As for me, my dreams to be a writer remained intact, but again, as in the past, I also recognized that our living situation required steady income. We lived in Marin County, California, not the cheapest place in the United States to be, and we were about to have a baby. Yes, I was all for carpe diem, but the sheer weight of reality, or what I thought was reality, conspired to hold me back once again from moving toward a career that was in my heart but not yet lodged in other places inside of me that I could turn to for practical purposes. In other words, I had no idea how to create income at the level of our requirements aside from working for someone else. Although I had been spectacularly unhappy in my career as an employee, working for a variety of businesses and agencies, I had always rationalized this sad record by saying that I had not made good choices about whom I worked for, rather than admitting to myself that I was someone who would be better off on my own.

To complicate matters even further, Diane and I were in the initial stages of developing a desire to live in Europe. She had already done so, as a high school student in London in the early seventies, and I had spent time there as a graduate student and later as a traveler. We had managed to arrange an extended period of time in Italy and elsewhere during our honeymoon, and we left Europe to return to the United States with the conviction that the future would see us go back to Italy to live. Was this the time?

It hardly seemed so. Moving to another country with no job possibilities and a wife who is five months pregnant didn't seem like the right thing to do. And then the financial considerations, which at the beginning of my unemployment seemed surmountable, started to worry me after a few weeks, and I found myself doing professionally what I had always done romantically, before Diane—I was getting involved by default. A position became available for which I was extremely qualified, and I and the corporation began to court each other. Before long, I found myself in intricate and extended negotiations over salary, benefits, profit sharing, and so on. It was an old and familiar dance, and I knew every step so well I could have been the choreographer.

Diane has great intuition, and there was something about the protracted interviews that I was forced to endure with the principals of the company that led her to conclude that the job was not going to bring me one iota closer to the vision I was developing for myself. Although the company was located close to home, and offered a service that was a decided help to high school students in need of a boost to their studies, there were problems that were just as real. I was choosing to ignore them, according to Diane, because I did not feel capable of seeking something that was more "me." I responded by saying that my dreams were still intact, but that we also needed the income, and I felt I could overcome the difficulties, make a positive contribution to the bottom line of the company, and make a lot of money. And of course, they wanted me—the telltale sign of relationship by default.

A few weeks after the job started, in March 1989, when I had already gotten my feet wet and the rest of me was rapidly plunging into the water, Diane and I were informed by the people from whom we were renting our house, the one we had moved into just weeks after Ethan died, that they were unhappy living in Annapolis and were moving back at the end of June. Diane was due in six weeks, and now we had to begin looking for a new place to live. The experience of being forced to leave the house we were renting made us ready to buy, and we looked at many alternatives, but nothing came close to what we had in mind. Then Diane walked into a place that she liked immediately, noticed a photo on a dresser, and said to our broker, "The man in that picture looks just like my chiropractor." It was her chiropractor, and negotiations to sell us the house went fairly smoothly from that point forward.

I wish I could say the same for my job. Although we had some early successes, by the summer everything was deteriorating. The program developed by the company for high school students was a summer program, and enrollments, as had been the case the year before—without my participation—were not meeting projections. It appeared that the company was headed for another loss, and in my position, these reversals were going to have an adverse impact on my life as well. All at once, the whole unhappy history of my career came gushing up from deep inside of me. The failures that I had experienced in past positions, the disappointments that had followed optimistic expectations, the misgivings I had had about where I was working and what I was doing overwhelmed me again. I was shocked, literally stunned, that I found myself in yet another professional relationship that I could not make right by sheer will alone.

Thoughts of living in Europe or being a writer were now as far from my consciousness as possible; in their place were thoughts of *survival,* and the prospects were terrifying. What was going to happen now? We had a baby, a mortgage, and a depleted savings account. We adored our house, and the thought of losing it was abhorrent to both of us. But the job was going so poorly. My effort there was tantamount to thrashing around in quicksand. The more I struggled, the harder I worked, the worse things got. Although I was not being blamed for the company's losses, the latter were nevertheless real and did not contribute to a sense of wellbeing or security.

I felt stuck, trapped. I was earning more money than I had ever earned before, and we were managing to carve out a lovely, comfortable life. How much of my dissatisfaction was me being me, and how much was the job? Why couldn't I just accept my good fortune and live like many others, who can put aside whatever reservations they have about their corporate lives and rejoice in the goodies—which in this case were manifest. What mattered more, the fact that I had an infant son whom I hardly knew, a house in Marin County I never had time to enjoy, and constant pressure that I could never shed, or the fact that I was a corporate executive earning nearly six figures? I had never been more professionally confused in my life.

I held on and muddled through. By October, despite the company's difficulties and my own reservations, my position seemed secure. My boss, who was the owner and founder, still considered me an asset. Although the company had again lost money, he felt that my work had in some ways prevented even greater losses. The fact that I had survived thus far, coupled with no visible way to earn a living as a writer or move to Italy, made me think that I should perhaps try to make this situation work after all. I even got a raise.

In the meantime, Diane founded True Partners, a matchmaking and relationship counseling service. She installed a second phone line in the house, designed a business card and stationery, and, with our six-month-old son, Julian, in tow, began organizing workshops and seminars to launch the company.

As the new decade approached, we visited with friends over the Christmas holiday, and it was in conversations with them that I realized, despite the raise and my instinct for corporate survival, how profoundly unhappy I was in my work. The previous year had been a terrible strain, and now I was facing the likelihood of a similar year. The company could not sustain another season of losses without folding, and so the pressure was likely to be even greater than it had been before. No amount of money could have made me feel that I was in the right "spot."

My friends were strong proponents of "personal growth." They believed that I was where I was because I had chosen to be there, and that before I could change my situation I had to change my thinking. They gave me a tape, "The Greatest Secret in the World," by Earl Nightingale, which relays a simple

message—that what you think is what you get. Think posi-
tively, and positive results ensue; think negatively, and life ful-
fills your expectations. I left with a sense of optimism for the
first time in a long time. My hope was based on the idea that I
was really in control of my life, and what I wanted to do I
could do. If I wanted to be a writer, I could be a writer. And if
I wanted to live in Italy, I could do that as well. While none of
this would happen without great effort, literally years of hard
work, at least I could begin the process by affirming, visualiz-
ing, imagining, seeing myself as a writer living in Italy, if that
is what I wanted.

I went to work every day and fulfilled my responsibilities
to the best of my ability, but in reality I lived a double life. My
mind was replete with images of writing and Italy. Diane and
I both made "dream" boards, collages of words and pictures
that reflected the life we desired. Mine was chock-full of ele-
gant fountain pens, sleek laptop computers, and all manner of
Italian scenes. I wrote down what I wanted in my life, and repeated it to myself at least fifty times a day—"I am a talented
artist, and, living in Italy with Diane and Julian, I am prospering by my writing and True Partners, and by bringing more
love into the world." I translated this into Italian and repeated
it even more. Each day, I couldn't wait for lunch. I quickly
gobbled a sandwich and walked all through the streets of
Marin County, saying over and over to myself the words I had
written and memorized.

I was trying to do my work at the same time my mind was
elsewhere, and I must admit it was difficult to keep everything straight. I thought about quitting my job, but it seemed,

especially in light of the faith my boss, Mark, had shown in me, like an irresponsible and ungrateful thing to do. I wanted to wait until something else materialized, something solid and wonderful, as we were not yet in a position to depend on Diane's efforts with True Partners.

One Sunday, discussing for the umpteenth time with Diane the depths of my professional unhappiness, we came up with an idea that would further the process of separation. I was to quit my job, but in my mind only, and then go into work the next day and see what happened. The effect was electrifying. I participated in the regular Monday department heads meeting, listening to the usual talk, and it all seemed so foreign to me, so distant and unrelated to anything that was going on inside me. It was almost as if I wasn't there at all, that my spirit had flown to some distant place and all that remained on the spot was the carcass that housed my body. But at the same time, I looked at a male colleague, across from whom I had sat month after month, and, paying only half attention to what he was saying, was suddenly re-minded of a single woman friend of Diane's. In a flash it came to me: we should introduce them. I approached him presently and asked if he was available and interested in meeting a woman—perhaps his true partner. He was. They met, fell in love, got married, and now have a two-year-old boy, who is our godson.

All the while, the company's fortunes slowly, almost tor-turously, continued to slide, and I could sense that something in my life needed to change. I wanted to leave my job, to be on my own, to spend more time with my family, and make a contribution to the world. At last my practical side was activated. I could do what I did in my job on a free-lance basis, freeing up valuable time to develop myself as a writer and join Diane in True Partners, which would benefit from both a male perspective and a lifelong interest in and fascination with relationships. Even though I could feel that change was imminent, a change that would probably see me without the steady income associated with a job, I was calm and optimistic. If I could survive the loss of my first child, only to be blessed shortly thereafter with a healthy son, then I could certainly endure whatever was to emerge professionally. I was now meeting people who had developed careers as consultants, and they were encouraging me to strike out on my own.

Just then Diane came to me with yet another idea to speed up the process. While she was meditating, it suddenly came to her that I should sit in our backyard, under Ethan's tree, for twenty minutes each day. I was to empty my mind as best I could, write one page in my journal after each session, and within one month my life would be completely different. I had known Diane long enough to be able to distinguish suggestions I could dismiss from those I had to follow, and I had no doubt that this was one of the latter. Later that afternoon I was meditating under Ethan's tree, and dutifully recorded what came to me immediately after. Here is a portion of it:

> Everything is in motion. This is the only true law of the universe. Nature never stands still. If one sits under a tree for more than a minute or two, one can't help but notice how changeable life is. The wind

moves the leaves on the branches and the branches on the trees. Things fall. Insects climb over everything. Clouds pass. The light is subtly different. The air stirs. Thoughts come and go.

I think about my life as an artist, a writer, and how I've not developed the many talents I possess, or rather how I have not had time to develop all of them at once. I think about the stories yet unwritten, and how much I will enjoy writing them when they are ready to come out.

The following week, on the evening of July 2, 1990, I answered the phone and heard the voice of my boss. The conversation was brief.

"Who was that?" asked Diane, after I had hung up.

"It was Mark," I replied.

"Why is he calling you now, at eight-thirty? He never calls you at home."

"He wants to have breakfast with me tomorrow morning."

"That's strange. I wonder what for."

"He's going to fire me."

"No, don't be silly. He's not going to fire you, not now, before the summer is over. Who would run the marketing?"

"No, Diane, really. As soon as I picked up the phone and heard his voice, I knew I was being fired."

Breakfast the next morning was just slightly longer than the phone conversation. My instinct the night before had been correct. I watched Mark squirm as he searched for a way to do what was clearly a difficult thing for him. Since I was quietly thrilled that this moment in my life had finally arrived, I let him off the hook early by saying that I understood, that it was the best thing for the company, and that I would manage. We shook hands and wished each other well.

I could hardly contain my joy. I was relieved of duty. I didn't even have to go in that day. Mark said I could come by the office the next morning, while people were preparing their Fourth of July barbecues and looking forward to fireworks, and pick up my stuff. I was home forty-five minutes after our meeting began, and was already planning the rest of my life. I gathered Diane and Julian together and we got in the car and drove north, without a destination, until we found a nice spot. We sat on the grass and laughed and cried and pledged that we would survive this as we had survived the death of Ethan. And we acknowledged that this was not only a loss, but a gain, and that in order for something new to be born, something old had to die.

I drove back in a kind of reverie. I couldn't believe how fortunate I was, or how quickly Diane's remedy, to meditate under Ethan's tree for one month, had worked. I pulled into the driveway, felt the warm summer California sun on my face, and celebrated my first day of independence. I washed the car.

Although the line from that day to the present has not been a straight one, my dreams have nonetheless been realized. Shortly after Independence Day, I became a consultant to a small company, an association that lasted for three years and was not only the perfect transition away from reliance on a job, but constituted one of the most lucrative, rewarding efforts of my career. I joined forces with Diane, and True Partners continued to grow, becoming one of the most respected introduction and relationship counseling services in California. Nine months after being fired, I woke up from a restless night and began to write down the things that made me happy, which eventually became my first published book, *How to Be Happier Day by Day: A Year of Mindful Actions*. That was followed by *How to Have More Love in Your Life: Everyday Actions for Nourishing Heart and Soul*, which came out two years later. *Anything Is Possible* is my third book, and I am writing a fourth, entitled *Stranded in the Land of Love: An American Family's Adventures in Italy*, as well as creating a TV series about Italy.

And I also live outside of Rome with Diane and the children, and am prospering by my writing and by bringing more love into the world. But that's a whole other story.